Beyond Agile

How To Run Faster, Smarter and Less Wasteful Projects

Beyond Agile: How To Run Faster, Smarter and Less Wasteful Projects

ISBN 978-0-6481612-0-2

Table of Contents

Preface

by Paul Shetler

Much ink has been spilled on the questions of efficiency and effectiveness in the software industry. An often-cited statistic suggests that between sixty-five and seventy-five per cent of all software that gets developed is never actually used. Others suggest that at least seventy per cent of software projects fail.

I don't know if those numbers are accurate or not, but what I do know is this: companies and organisations are slowly beginning to realise the existential nature of the challenge that digital hypercompetition poses to them.

What do I mean by this? I mean that executives are witnessing creative destruction - the process through which something new brings about the demise of what preceded it - happening in real time, right in their backyards. They're seeing the destruction wrought by disruptors on incumbents in industries like music, media and retail, and they can no longer afford to see the world through rose-coloured glasses. The writing's on the wall.

A 2015 global survey conducted by the *MIT Sloan Management Review* found nearly ninety per cent of managers and executives anticipate that their industries will be disrupted by digital trends to a 'great or moderate extent.' But here's the catch: only forty-four per cent thought their company was adequately prepared for disruption

Taking action in the face of hypercompetition is hard, and 'digital transformation' is often touted as its silver bullet. Company boards are bombarded with offers of advice from large vendors and consultants, all claiming to have the 'secret' to unlocking innovation. But settling for panaceas like 'innovation studios' and other lipstick solutions is not enough to secure a company's digital future.

For a transformation to be effective, it needs to go deep into the business and change the very nature of how that business operates. This requires three steps:

Redesign internal structures

The most successful companies in the digital age are product-focussed. Product management (which I define as the ongoing improvement of a product based on changing understanding of user needs) should be the core function in a company, and ancillary functions should support delivery of brilliant products in real-time.

For this structure to work, IT has to shift from the start-and-stop paradigm of project management and instead work towards to continuous iteration under the direction of a product manager. Successful companies release updates to their products hundreds or even thousands of times a day, not once every six months.

Leadership and role clarity plays a role too. A great digital product isn't just a user interface; it is an ensemble of great people, processes, policies and systems. It doesn't make sense for companies to split product responsibilities between a Chief Digital Officer for the front-end and a Chief Information Officer providing the backend. Organisations need a single Chief Digital and Information Officer (CDIO) with oversight for consolidated digital service delivery, which is orchestrated by the product management function.

Abolishing the digital/IT split in this manner is also useful from a product lifecycle perspective. It allows the CDIO to match people's aptitudes to the methodologies suited to different stages of product development. Simon Wardle, advisor and researcher for Leading Edge Forum, breaks digital workforces down into three categories of talent:

1. Pioneers. In the last century, these were the people who invented the first digital computer. They're comfortable working on novel, user-facing problems where experimentation and rapid learning is essential to understanding user needs and reducing risk, usually in small teams bearing full responsibility for product delivery. They are innovators who are at ease with lean and Agile methodologies,

and they'll grow frustrated if tasked with solving only well-defined problems.

2. Settlers. Settlers take ownership of products as they begin to scale. They fine-tune them into broader-based, commercialised products that are ready to be manufactured at scale. They turned the first ever digital computer into the household microcomputers of the 1980s and introduced a generation of people to computer science.

3. Town planners. These are the people who take settlers' products and industrialise them into highly profitable and commoditised products that take advantage of economies of scale. Their talents lie in perfecting and creating platforms from existing products. They're comfortable engineering solutions to well-defined problems using highly structured methods.

We can't (and shouldn't) expect digital workers to be all things to all people. Their skills and mindsets correspond to specific points in a product's lifecycle. Allocating them to the roles that fit their aptitudes and attitudes makes the best use of employees' skills, and enables a conveyor belt to move products from ideation through to commercialisation and then 'platformisation.'

Tackle the Square of Despair

Too many companies suffer from what I call the 'Square of Despair,' and tackling it is the second step towards achieving true transformation. This square is made up of four structural forces that collude to resist change, especially within large organisations.

1. Inappropriate procurement that stems from years of outsourcing and deskilling. Organisations that rely heavily on outsourcing turn their IT teams into vendor relationship managers instead of makers, and they split the delivery and design of their services between multiple vendors. This is a problem because it puts vendors in a position of having to fix a project's scope at a point when they have the least information to do so: when they first put out a request for tender, or before building a prototype and seeing what users really expect from a product.

2. Inappropriate governance that slows down delivery. Heavy, waterfall-style governance is used on products for which it is ill-suited, increasing the risk of failure. Too many steering committees and programme boards are expected to understand the status and intent of a product from a one hundred-page risk document sent immediately before a governance meeting. Even companies practising Agile are doing this, though Agile has its own risk mitigation elements and doesn't need the governance of another method designed for a different type of problem added to it.

3. Broken IT that leaves employees to use their state-of-the-art smartphones for recreation, while they wait up to half an hour for their PC to boot up at work. Broken IT can also refer to IT that's wrapped in layers upon layers of contracts and systems integrators. As I've said before: if you need to negotiate with vendors to access your own resources, then your IT management is broken.

4. Inappropriate funding which is based on the old model of heavy capital expenditure and outsourcing is another significant problem. For the early stages of products led by pioneers, it is wrong to have funding that's conditional on claiming certainty from the the start. A drip feed funding model is more appropriate; after a couple of sprints, leaders can decide whether to continue to fund based on outcomes delivered. For platforms, where by definition there will be have a well specified requirement, it is essential for a business case and set funding to be developed to remove ambiguity.

Tackling the Square of Despair means making procurement fast, nimble and chunking it down into smaller purchases. This allows access to innovative solutions from start-ups and small-to-medium enterprises; that's why government agencies have developed Australia's Digital Marketplace and the UK's G-Cloud.

Most importantly, tackling the Square of Despair means reversing the deskilling and learnt helplessness of the organisation on which it feeds. The reason why so many firms rely on contractors and heavy governance is ultimately because they don't trust their employees to deliver anymore. In too many companies, that's for good reason: a recent report published by the Boston Consulting Group found digital capability and training is lacking across industries like retail, financial services and consumer goods. It's clear that there's a need for digital training at every level of an organisation, including the boardroom and executive suite.

Demonstrate political will

This is the last step towards effective transformation. Transformation can be painful and there will be challenges and resistance, especially from people in the legacy parts of an organisation.

That cannot be used as an excuse to pull back from deep-seated transformation and turn to surface-level solutions. Transformation by consensus or by occasional hackathon will not work, because transformation is not iteration from a low baseline: it requires making fundamental changes to an organisation's structure and processes.

Where to from here?

I know what you're thinking. How can organisations go about doing all of those things? The answer depends on the organisation. Every business is different, and the role of a business's technology function depends on its needs and ambition levels.

Here's the bottom line: every company has the ability to transform IT and improve its competitive positioning in today's challenging market. And the ideas and methodologies outlined in this book can help you do that.

Agile has changed how we work in the digital space, without a doubt. But Agile on its own is not enough to tackle the problem of survival in the face of hypercompetition. There are a few reasons for this, outlined later in the book, but it comes down to these realities: Agile is not a solution for every problem, and most companies don't really know what Agile is anyway.

This book is the story of a company called 3wks, but it is also the story of a few people who are trying to effect change in the way we create products, without reinventing the wheel. It is the story of progress. It is the story of life beyond today's Agile practices and yet, ironically, it's about delivering on the tenets in the Agile Manifesto - but in a more accessible and repeatable way.

In this book you will learn a few things:

- Why product and software development is the way it is;

- Why Agile and other lean methodologies aren't enough on their own to survive in the digital age; and

- What it will really take to make your organisation fast, resilient and capable of innovation.

The methodology outlined in this book is one that will help you redesign internal structures, defeat the Square of Despair and overcome resistance to change. But most of all it will help you start delivering products with a faster time to market, and with less wastage.

Waiting any longer to embrace digital change means exposing your organisation - and your employees - to the risk of being driven out of the market entirely. Transformation is difficult but it's essential if you want to survive these next few years. So read this book, and take notes. You'll need them.

On the origins of 3wks

In the tiny village of Otterlo, south-east of Amsterdam, a relatively small museum occupies a section of the Hoge Veluwe National Park.

Called the Kröller-Müller Museum, this place boasts the second-largest collection of paintings by the influential Dutch post-impressionist, Vincent van Gogh. Its collection rivals that of the eminent Van Gogh Museum in Amsterdam, and includes the 1887 painting 'Patch of grass.'

Van Gogh is said to have painted Patch of grass after arriving in Paris in 1886 and encountering the Impressionists for the first time. Examining the painting with the naked eye, you can certainly see elements of Van Gogh's signature vivid style, as well as the calling cards of Impressionism: light colours, deft brushwork, new painting techniques. What you can't see, however, is a woman's head.

Beneath Patch of grass, on the very same canvas, is a portrait of a Dutch peasant woman likely painted by van Gogh in 1884. This painting, discovered by researchers using a cutting-edge X-ray fluorescence mapping technique, is a stark contrast to Patch of grass. Its palette is dark and evocative of van Gogh's old-fashioned, pre-Paris ways. To anyone who is not an art historian, it barely looks like a van Gogh.

What Patch of grass shows is that nobody - even the Old Masters - started out a success. Every piece of work, whether it be a painting, a book or a software programme, is the product of experience and learning. Van Gogh is believed to have painted over at least a third of his older works. Picasso and Rembrandt did it too.

In this first chapter, we will focus the figurative X-rays on our own lives and uncover the people, projects and formative moments that shaped the eventual 3wks methodology. The influence of the Impressionists is lost on us, but the influence of others is palpable.

Early days

San Saba, the twenty-first rione of Rome, is a deeply charming and understated place.

Enwreathed by the tree-lined Viale delle Terme di Caracalla, remnants of the Rome's opulent past - the Baths of Caracalla, and the Circo Massimo - draw modest crowds. There is an orange orchard and numerous churches, theatres and museums with fine belvederes. It's a quiet place, devoid of the city's usual mayhem.

It's perhaps for this reason that the in 1949, the Member States of the United Nations voted to officially relocate the Food and Agriculture Organisation (FAO) to Rome. Headquartered in a building that once housed the Ministry of Italian Africa, the FAO would serve as a repository of knowledge and guidance, helping governments of developing nations ensure adequate nutrition and food security for their populations. It was (and remains) a controversial organisation, and one that has gone through several transformations and internal restructures since its inception.

Andrew first visited the FAO building in San Saba in the early 1970s, when he was just a kid. His father, a rocket scientist (or 'aeronautical engineer', as he prefered to be called) looking to escape defence work in the United Kingdom, had taken a job there and relocated the family from Britain to Rome. It was Andrew's first encounter with a 'modern' data centre.

At that time, computers and data centres took up entire buildings. One of the very first data centres, EINAC (or Electronic Numerical Integrator and Computer, built in 1964) housed more than seventeen thousand vacuum tubes, seven thousand crystal diodes and ten thousand capacitors. The whole thing took up eighteen hundred square feet of floor space (which is roughly the size of your average tennis court) and consumed one hundred and fifty kilowatts of power.

Andrew was amazed by the sheer scale of what he saw at the FAO building. Rows of cabinets and server racks upon server racks housed the organisation's vast datasets that had been, since 1961, collating information on everything from livestock production and trade to fertiliser and pesticide use. It was momentous. Impressive. And a little bit boring.

Data centres, like other information storage facilities - libraries and museums, for example - are fundamentally boring places. They are quiet, save the gentle hum of lightbulbs or computers, temperature-controlled and utilitarian. And yet as human beings, we're fascinated by them. They are symbols of human capability; reliquaries filled with data that speaks to our future successes and failures, as well as those of the past.

None of this occurred to Andrew on that first trip to San Saba, of course. But that feeling of immense possibility, that everything you needed to succeed was in front of you, would stay with him forever.

For Andrew, the story of 3wks starts in San Saba because he believes being exposed to technology so early in life is what inspired his love for it. His father, who was working in data processing (a relatively nascent and uber exciting field at the time) would bring home early PCs and pseudo-computers and take Andrew to his office to see servers, computers and things he'd only ever seen in James Bond films. It was extremely exciting and appealed to the academic side of his personality, but it also stirred a love for technology that has inspired many of Andrew's ideas and actions throughout his life.

But while Andrew was roaming the racks in San Saba, Paul was enjoying a rather idyllic childhood in the south of England. His father was too an engineer and had moved from a mining town in the Welsh valleys to West Sussex, where he'd met his wife and developed interests in everything from jet planes to Jaguars. Living in the remote Sussex countryside with two siblings and a myriad of pets, Paul wasn't touring data centres or UN buildings. He was tending to horses.

 Paul had gotten into horse riding at a young age. Every day, before going to school, he would rise before dawn to muck out and feed his horse. Nothing teaches you about compassion, responsibility and understanding the needs of others quite like horse riding, he says.

He stayed in West Sussex throughout his school years and despite struggling with exams, he made it into Chichester College and pursued engineering with the intention of joining the family business. Andrew, meanwhile, had set sail for Sydney.

When he was ten years old, Andrew's family emigrated to Australia on what was supposed to be the final voyage of the SS Galileo Galilei, the Lloyd Triestino ship that had been the workhorse for Italians migrating to Australia for over a decade. The trip took roughly six weeks in total and in the end, the ship wasn't decommissioned. It was remodelled and renamed several times before eventually catching fire and sinking in 1999 (fortunately, without casualties).

By the 1990s Andrew's family had moved to a place called Yeppoon, a quintessential coastal town in Central Queensland. They stayed there until Andrew graduated high school, after which he went on to pursue a Bachelor of Business at Central Queensland University (CQU). His father, who had left his career in data processing and become a lecturer, had actually designed the course for CQU a few years before. There's an insight in there somewhere about the immeasurable impact our parents have on our lives; Umberto Eco believed that what we become depends on what our fathers teach us at odd moments.

Psychologists have long believed that our childhood experiences shape who we are as adults. Looking back on the early days, we - Paul and Andrew - can probably thank our childhoods for teaching us one thing: resilience. Resilience in the face of change, and resilience in the face of uncertainty and ambiguity. Both would become important in our journey towards 3wks.

The projects and the people

Of course, it's the projects and the people we've worked with throughout our careers that have had the most significant impact on the development of beliefs and working practices. For Andrew, the most formative projects came by way of EY, Sony, Walmart and Dixons Retail. For Paul, it was the people and projects at Myson Group, Merchants and Dimension Data that had the most impact. In this section, we'll each recount our experiences - and why they mattered - in our own words.

In Andrew's words

I graduated university at the end of 1987 and started work the next year at an Australian telecommunications company in Brisbane. I spent twelve months there, totally brain dead and bored out of my mind, until I was headhunted by Arthur Young (which became Ernst & Young, and is now EY).

I spent a decade at Ernst & Young working in what they called 'enterprise resource planning systems' - in other words, things like SAP and Oracle. My particular flavour was Oracle and most of our clients (with a few exceptions) were implementing large-scale accounting systems. We worked with people like the Queensland Government, big electrical companies, and a couple of new private sector organisations like Optus, and most of what we did could best be described as firefighting. We were getting involved in projects where things had gone wrong and it was our job to rescue them, usually on a ridiculous timeline with an impossible deadline.

It sounds horrible but if I'm honest, that kind of environment motivated me. I realised early on that I'm something of an 'efficiency nut' (another thing I may have inherited from my father) and I relished the challenge of fixing things and delivering outcomes on tight schedules. I didn't realise it then, but my experiences at Ernst & Young were laying the foundations for what would eventually become the 3wks methodology.

Ten years after joining the company I found myself in a director role; I was a partner-in-training-wheels, if you will. And at that point I found myself having a lot of arguments with the management team.

I had proven it was possible to put Oracle Financials into a company in about a quarter of the time it would normally take. I had also developed and formalised two rapid methodologies - Project Rescue and Package-enabled Process Reengineering - which formed part of Ernst & Young's trademarked software development methodology, Navigator. In my view, being able to deliver projects in half the time (or less) than we expected was awesome.

Others, unfortunately, didn't see it that way. The managing partner called me a lunatic because I was effectively wanting to cut the company's revenues by half or three-quarters on every project I ran.

That was the point I realised that a career in consulting wasn't for me, so I quit. I decided to shift my focus back to software development - something I had been missing terribly since the early move to package implementation with EY. Perhaps I'd reached a certain age, or perhaps I'd been more unnerved by my experience at Ernst & Young than I'd realised. Whatever it was, I was feeling like I really needed a break from my career.

So I indulged in a little backpacking through the UK and Europe, mainly visiting relatives. I tried and struggled to get a bartending job in London and somehow, I ended up trying my hand at cold calling (or 'telesales' as we call it today). During what was to become the shortest job of my career I met my wife, Alison, and realised I needed a bit more dosh to wine and dine her - so I joined a boutique consulting firm in London and spent a while there before returning to Australia.

The French have a saying: you often meet your fate on the road you take to avoid it. I had left Ernst & Young and renounced a career in consulting, and in a bid to avoid that path I made lots of choices (and took on many projects) that eventually led me to set up my own consulting firm, 3wks.

The first of those choices was to move, once again, back to the United Kingdom and really switch my focus to digital. The dot-com boom was just starting to take off and I found myself working in project management, mostly in what you'd call digital projects (back then it was called a variety of things: web, online, ecommerce, etcetera).

I spent most of 1998 working for Robert Fleming & Co in Luxembourg, where I got to play around with a lot of early Java and web technologies. We had to figure out how to rewrite a fund management system or 'unit management system' for the fund, and the project involved fascinating technologies like fingerprint scanners on laptops and government-grade encryption.

I worked on several other projects, mostly application development projects, for financial institutions like Credit Suisse until 1999. That's when I joined Sony.

This was where the seeds of the 3wks methodology really started to germinate. I'd been brought in as part of a small team tasked with developing multiple online, self-service solutions intended for use in product distribution throughout Europe. In a six-week period we were able to roll out a whole multilingual, multi-jurisdictional, multi-currency ecommerce application that managed the flow of products from Sony's central fulfilment system into every single one of its retail stores in Europe. The project was highly successful, and the vendor of the product (Broadvision) cited it as its most impressive reference implementation in Europe for about ten years.

My time at Sony can only be described as formative. I learned so much there, and it's where I started to put a lot of my ideas (which would eventually evolve into the 3wks methodology) down onto paper. I even experienced several epiphanies. I realised, for example, that the most fun jobs were the ones where you had a small team (about three to four people) and a clear objective. I also realised just how important a 'golden sponsor' was to a successful project. If you were able to sit next to the person who was paying for your time, who was emotionally invested, and for whom the project was a real labour of love, then you could move mountains with very little in the way of manpower and resources.

So I had found my footing in digital and the 3wks methodology was half-baked. I left Sony and joined a startup called Silver Network Logistics which, interestingly, wasn't an internet startup. It was a logistics venture specialising in 'responsive delivery' - i.e. next-hour delivery and scheduled delivery. We built a customer-integrated order and fleet route management system using an early variant of scrum, with weekly iterative development and weekly sponsor meetings. It was a great team and a great company, but unfortunately the bursting of the dot-com bubble saw the end of it. Silver Network Logistics wasn't a tech company, but many of its customers were.

In the wake of 2001 I worked with Walmart and built its first online (and digital TV) customer ordering platform for the company's UK arm, Asda. The product integrated with in-store picking systems and at one point enabled people to order their groceries via satellite TV. We did it by assembling Open Source software using extreme programming techniques, and I spent that time further refining my own methodology and ideas (especially around things like recruitment, small releases, team structures and motivation).

And then came Dixons Retail. Once one of the largest consumer electronics retailers in Europe (and parent to well-known brands like PC World and Currys Digital), Dixons was where I experienced my Second Awakening - the first being at Sony.

The job I had been tasked with was almost inconsequential in their grand scheme of things, but it was one of the biggest Agile projects the company had ever undertaken - and one of the biggest projects I've ever run. I was recruited as a project manager via a friend of a friend and they asked me to 'rescue' the £ 70 million 'Eclipse' programme, which was aimed at replacing point-of-sale (POS) and in-store systems at more than one thousand stores across the UK. That's thirteen thousand tills and in-store PCs.

We started by restructuring the one hundred person programme and selecting a new supplier for the software build. We worked with Martin Fowler, one of the signatories of the Agile Manifesto, and used a lot of extreme programming (XP) techniques. We moved from first release to a three-store trial in under three months.

I learned a lot from the way Dixons ran itself as a business, and the project gave me a great opportunity to observe the XP community and see what works, and what doesn't. But the real learning for me was in the business side of things.

I was fascinated by how Dixon's funded projects and approached problem solving. They sincerely engaged with problems instead of trying to solve them in one massive hit, an approach I hadn't really seen in my career before. A lot of the ideas developed in the 3wks methodology (and in this book) around business engagement, people management and incremental rollout all come from my experience with Dixon's Retail.

I built on these ideas over successive jobs with British Telecom and then Evoxus, the UK's first digital-first telco. I had several great mentors during this time, and I was exposed to big transformational projects in which we were able to significantly impact the value of the companies I worked with.

I was enjoying my work, but in 2008 my wife and I made the decision to move back to Australia to give our kids some exposure to the things I'd loved about the country as I'd grown up. I joined Insurance Group Australia (IAG) as a project manager and established an Agile delivery capability to implement a digital-self service solution for a range of personal insurance products across four brands.

We were using extreme programming methodologies again and experimenting with interesting stuff, like automated user acceptance testing. But over time I found myself getting more and more frustrated yet again. History doesn't repeat itself, but it often does rhyme.

Having tasted the good life at places like Dixons Retail and Sony, where we'd been able to achieve great things with few resources, I was spoiled. I was trying to apply the philosophies and learnings I'd gathered overseas in an environment where it just wasn't working. I could see what was possible, but it was unattainable in an organisation where projects are funded on a yearly basis and you have to prepare a business case for tens of millions of dollars for an activity that should really only cost one.

But the main reason it wasn't working had nothing to do with funding or bureaucracy, though they were factors. The main reason my methodologies weren't working was structure; we were always working for the wrong people and we were working too late in decision cycle, when the solution had already been cast in concrete by others.

In all of the projects at IAG and elsewhere, my teams worked for IT. And while Agile was working for IT, I realised it was never going to work for the enterprise. Why? Because IT are the one group of people who don't understand the business imperatives. They aren't operational.

During this time I was setting up an Agile community at the request of Roy Singham, founder and Chairman of ThoughtWorks Inc. Singham wanted an 'Agile centre of gravity' in Australia that wasn't ThoughtWorks, so we created a meet-up and built a community of two thousand people. It was energising and encouraging to see so many people interested in Agile.

But it wasn't long before I found myself facing the same old frustrations. I realised that while these forums were being attended by IT people, we as a group were never going to solve the problem of:

1. applying Agile at scale and

2. applying Agile in enterprises to maximum effect.

To do those things we'd have to get out of our IT bubble and actually engage with - gasp - business people. And engaging with business people required either having an internal group dedicated to that engagement, or a completely separate company - like 3wks.

In Paul's words

When I left school, I had every intention of following in my father's footsteps, becoming an engineer, and joining the family business. But for whatever reason, I didn't.

I completed the first two years of a degree course at Chichester College and decided to go to the south of France. I wasn't sure what I was going to do with my career, but I met some incredibly interesting people - one of whom had a connection with somebody at a company called Myson Group in the UK.

By the time I returned to the UK I had decided that what I really wanted to do was get into marketing and advertising. Through my acquaintance I secured an interview at Myson and joined the company as a sales trainee. It was my first proper job.

It wasn't very glamorous. Myson was a manufacturer of heating and ventilating equipment, and after completing a TACK International sales training course (one of many such courses designed by George and Alfred Tack, whose company also manufactured and sold ventilation and heating equipment in the early 20th century) I was assigned to a senior salesperson.

Together we travelled around the countryside, selling equipment to distributors, plumbers and whoever would buy from us.

I did this for about a year before applying for a vacancy in the marketing department, which got me into the thing I was most interested in: marketing and advertising. It was in this role that I really started learning about things like public relations and product marketing; Myson had a catalogue of around one hundred and fifty products, and I wrote descriptions and sales brochures for at least half of them.

But it's funny how fate takes a hold of a situation, isn't it?. I'd been learning the trade in my first marketing role at Myson for less than year before ten out of the fifteen people in the department were made redundant. I survived the cull, and before I knew it the Managing Director was offering me the role of marketing manager.

John Coyle, a great PR and marketing communications professional (who sadly passed in 2006) had taught me the basics of marketing and given me the confidence to take on a management role. So, being in my early twenties and not knowing any better, I took the job.

I spent the next three years learning on the job, managing a team and overseeing quite a substantial advertising budget that spanned national television and print channels. It was a steep learning curve in many respects, but those four years at Myson gave me foundational skills that I would draw on throughout my career.

Working at Myson was enjoyable, but something told me that manufacturing was never going to set the world on fire. I wanted to expand my horizons and take the skills I'd acquired and transition into the IT sector. So I started applying for jobs, and secure a role with Hoskyns.

At the time, Hoskyns (which was eventually purchased by Cap Gemini Sogeti) was the preeminent systems house in the United Kingdom. It was here that I worked alongside Group Marketing Director Richard Holway, a man who would become one of my first mentors and a lifelong friend.

Richard is an extraordinary man, and I credit him with furthering the development of my marketing and consulting skills at that stage of my life and beyond. He probably knows more about the development and growth of the IT services sector than anyone in the UK, and he made it possible for me to apply what I'd learned in manufacturing to the IT sector. Under his guidance, I began to learn about the sophistication of marketing services and build on my previous experiences. It was an important time in my career for personal and professional development.

Eventually, Richard left Hoskyns for Wootton Jeffreys, a smaller, specialist systems house that worked in the transportation sector. He poached me from Hoskyns and I too worked at Wootton Jeffreys for nearly four years, learning more and more about the importance of a customer-focussed approach to selling and marketing. It was at Hoskyns and Wootton Jeffreys that I really began to think about customer centricity and bringing customers and 'users' into processes, sowing the seeds for the 3wks methodology.

Richard and I shared a passion for creating interesting and successful services in the IT sector, so we set up an organisation called Holway Scott communications and sold our marketing services to the IT industry. We won our first client, Apple, in 1987 and helped the company establish its business-to-business sales team in the United Kingdom.

My early years in marketing had taught me the importance of maintaining a focus on customer needs and wants, and my foray into into consulting gave me the opportunity to get inside the workings of big organisations. I observed how they took products and services to market, what processes and systems they used, the challenges they faced and how they adapted (or failed to adapt) to the ever-changing world. These learnings formed the basis of much of my later thinking around team structures, processes and change resistance - all of which would inform my experience at 3wks.

When the 1990s rolled around Richard decided he wanted to pursue other opportunities, so I sold my part of our business to Merchants Group and we parted ways. I'd been in contact with Merchants a few times throughout my career (usually because they were trying to sell me something) and when they heard the news that Holway Scott were parting ways, they made a grab for the business.

Merchants was a contact centre and outsourcing business with a dream of establishing its own internal consulting capability. It was here that I met Robert D'Aubigny, the creator of the controversial Exegesis Programme in the 1970s. Robert had founded a telesales company called Programmes Ltd., which went on to become a successful telemarketing business and a forerunner of Merchants Group. With Robert I learned more about people, the power of the individual and the importance of being present than I had anywhere else.

I spent a good chunk of the 1990s working with Merchants, growing its consulting proposition around customer service. This was where I really began thinking of customer experience as a principal point of value. By 1996 we had grown the consulting business to around forty people, and then the company was sold to Dimension Data. Myself and my team were made redundant, and I found my next opportunity in the form of VIA International.

VIA is a boutique consulting firm that, at the time, helped companies find and forge routes to market for new products and services. I joined as a business development director and spent four amazing years travelling and learning about how organisations trade with customers abroad, in places like Hong Kong and the United States. It was my first real taste of delivering customer experiences in new, exciting contexts.

The opportunity to advance my learning in that area came by way of a project for the King of Jordan, of all people. At the behest of a former colleague I travelled to Jordan and spent three months there preparing a report for the King, who wanted to present Jordan as a prime location for contact centres and offshore businesses to the International Monetary Fund (IMF). We looked at everything from infrastructure integrity and the talent pool to security and technology; in the end, the IMF gave Jordan half a billion in investment capital to attract companies like SAP and Microsoft to the region.

When my time in Jordan came to an end, my colleague asked me what I was doing to do next. I said I had no idea - which was true - and he suggested I join Dimension Data's contact centre business as a General Manager. At this point I'd not had much experience in tech or contact centres, and I was perplexed by the offer; I wasn't a tech person, so why me? The reason, apparently, was that they needed a business person. And that's where I learned my next big lesson: tech skills are essential in big tech projects, but a bit of business acumen goes a long way too.

For three years I ran Dimension Data's contact centre tech practice in the UK, which quadrupled in size and added a whole series of new technology capabilities to its portfolio over time. Eventually the company offered me another job, this time back in Merchants Group as their head of consulting. My team was small - we had only five full-time consultants - but we recruited a large group of associates to help us out. That model and team structure was something that I carried into 3wks.

The work we were doing was twofold: call centre optimisation (improving efficiency and effectiveness) and building customer service operations from scratch. That included sourcing technology and people as well as developing strategies and processes. We worked with quite a few different organisations, but our first big project took us to Bahrain.

Bahrain is a place I'd never considered travelling to and I admit I was intimidated when when presented with the project. But Adam Foster, who had been my boss at Dimension Data and Merchants Group for some eight years, convinced me to take the plunge. Adam was an exceptional leader and had a knack for getting the best out of every member of his team. He made it look effortless, and I think I learned more about effective management (and what makes a high-performing team successful) in those eight years than i had in the previous fifteen. There's the next learning: don't be afraid to take risks, and believe in the people you have around you.

So I took a team out to Bahrain to build joint venture with the Bahraini government: a contact centre. Part of the 'eGovernment vision,' the contact centre would serve the public as well as operate as a commercial enterprise offering outsourced customer service to Arabic-speaking businesses.

It was an operation built from scratch. Starting in 2009, we found a location, sourced the people, designed the processes, introduced the technology and got the whole thing up and running. Within two years, we were ready to hand over the operation.

I hate to be dramatic, but this project was life changing for me. It made me understand the value and importance of seeing things from a different cultural perspective. I won't say it was without its challenges - we were there during the early years of the Arab Spring, after all - but it was profoundly transformative. I didn't experience anything quite like it until a few years later.

I was sitting in my pyjamas on Christmas Eve in 2013 when I was asked to present to the management team at Reliance Industries and comment on the state of the call centre market in Asia and India. Reliance had reached out to us because we had previously published the Global Contact Centre Benchmarking Report, and they wanted to know more. So we obliged, and we presented to them the findings of our research; there was a massive opportunity for organisations - particularly in India - to take a lead role in providing world-class customer service operations.

Reliance liked what we had told them, and invited us to Mumbai in the first week of January to run a five-day workshop in the leadup to the company's next 'major programme.' Not knowing anything about this programme, we got on the plane and delivered the workshop as asked. The end product? A fully-fledged strategy for implementing a customer service operation designed to service nearly three hundred million customers in India.

We were floored by the experience. Working with Reliance Industries and encountering Indian culture first hand was more eye-opening than we could have imagined, in the best way possible. I was thrilled to have had the opportunity just to present and facilitate a workshop, so you can imagine how we felt when Reliance asked us to quote on the project we had 'theoretically' mapped out for them.

And so, the last sixteen or so months in my career at Dimension Data were spent working on an extraordinary project: the creation of the 4G network in India in collaboration with Reliance Industries, the telecom company owned by the enigmatic Mukesh Ambani. It was arguably the biggest infrastructure project in India since the railways, and we built its customer service operation from scratch. We set up the human resources department, designed and implemented business processes, and we did it all over a fifteen month period. The service launched in September of 2016 and at scale will employ in excess of twelve thousand agents in sixteen different centres across India.

Working in the customer services and call centre industry taught me the importance of people, culture and teams in delivering successful projects. Merchants Group is a world leader in high quality customer engagement - we wrote the book on how to run world class customer services - and subsequent projects in the UK, Bahrain and India reinforced everything I'd learned there in those the early years. If it weren't for those projects and the people who worked on them, I would be a very different person.

I think the main thing I've learned from all these experiences was this: if solution providers don't put customers and end users in the forefront of design and development, the solutions they deliver will never be fully successful. Like Andrew, throughout my career I had become increasingly frustrated with how long it took to deliver working software solutions. I could see the waste and compounded inefficiencies arising from protracted development cycles, which never involved end users and customers throughout the development phase. These frustrations and learnings are what attracted me to 3wks and the 3wks methodology. And they're still what drive me today.

The moral of the ongoing story

When Andrew left IAG for News Corp, he found a lot of support for the 3wks philosophy and methodology. He experimented with it in a couple of projects and then with permission from some key people, like the Head of Digital Platforms and the Head of National Systems, 3wks quoted for its first project as a fledgling independent company.

News Corp trusted the people that had joined 3wks and saw that by creating an A-team in a separate organisation, more could be achieved with less money - especially with cloud technology in its arsenal. 3wks delivered its first job (initially quoted at $3.9 million) successfully, and at $1.9 million under budget.

Here's the thing: 3wks wasn't born in a vacuum or snapped into existence by some cosmic event. It is the product of years of projects, experiences and learnings. It is our proverbial Patch of grass. We, Paul and Andrew, have told the story of our personal journeys because the journey deserves the credit. Without it, we wouldn't be here.

If you've learned anything from this chapter, let it be this:

1. **You don't have to be a genius or a programming wizard to make a difference.** Neither of us have ever been star programmers or serial entrepreneurs.

2. **Even van Gogh made mistakes.** Learning by osmosis and taking lessons from others, French Impressionists or otherwise, is more important than getting things right the first time.

3. **Persistence and grit make all the difference.** You can be the smartest person in the world and it will mean nothing if you're not willing to work; Arthur Ashe, the Grand Slam title-winning American tennis player, said that success is a journey, not a destination. Doing something and keeping at it is what makes for a successful outcome.

As people we're conditioned to think that some things, like entrepreneurs or industry game-changers, are born and not made. That's not true for software, nor is it true for anything else.

In the next chapters of this book, we'll explore the people, ideas and methodologies that have shaped software and brought us to the version of the oil painting we're working on today: the 3wks methodology. Maybe one day we'll paint over it, and maybe we won't. Either way, we hope you learn something from it.

The 3wks methodology

The arrival of the Agile Manifesto at the beginning of the 21st century signalled the end of an era. A refreshing new methodology, Agile was set to disrupt a pattern that the software development industry had grown all too weary of: big ideas, even bigger projects, and a lot of waste, frustration and embarrassment.

And for the most part, Agile has been disruptive. The Agile revolution has changed software delivery, largely for the better. If nothing else, it's put the notion of agility - the idea of moving faster and being more nimble - on the radar of historically slow moving organisations. Indeed, a survey of more than six hundred software development professionals by Hewlett Packard Enterprise found that two-thirds of companies now describe themselves as either 'pure Agile' or 'leaning toward Agile.' Agile, it seems, is the new normal.

But we don't need surveys to tell us this. You can see it all around you. Even within the most glacial of organisations you'll find teams having their daily or weekly standup meeting, or performing their 'Agile ceremonies.' The walls are covered in scrum boards and technicolour Agile cards, and meeting rooms are occupied by small groups attempting a great new thing called 'design thinking.' Agile is everywhere.

Or so it seems. In reality, most organisations aren't practising Agile proper. What they're performing is just a more glamorous form of waterfall, dressed up for the new millennium. And their projects typically look like this:

1. A quarter of the budget is spent on architecting and setting up infrastructure;

2. Much time is spent developing user stories, defining requirements and planning. As a result, iterations are only pushed for testing and feedback in the twilight hours of a sprint;

3. The project accumulates a lot of technical debt, and the pile of requirements and user stories that can't be actioned on just keeps rising;

4. A huge amount of time is allocated at the end of the project for a thing often called 'user acceptance testing'; and

5. Development happens in iterations, but implementation still only happens at the end of the project.

We see organisations spending huge amounts of time and money following a set of working practices that, in the end, deliver the same results as waterfall. And with that often comes a lot of collateral damage in the form of documentation, elaborate delivery processes (like the Scaled Agile Framework, or SAFe) and, of course, software that just sucks.

A typical project

Development happens in iterations, but implementation still only happens at the end of the project.

A quarter of the budget is spent on architecting and setting up infrastructure;

Much time is spent developing user stories, defining requirements and planning. As a result, iterations are only pushed for testing and feedback in the twilight hours of a sprint;

The project accumulates a lot of technical debt, and the pile of requirements and user stories that can't be actioned on just keeps rising;

A huge amount of time is allocated at the end of the project for a thing often called 'user acceptance testing';

Agile as it is practised today is an effective way to deliver features, but so is waterfall and a host of other methodologies. This is perhaps why Andrew Hunt, one of the original authors if the Agile Manifesto, announced the death of Agile in 2015. Writing on his blog, Hunt says:

> *"The word 'Agile' has become sloganised; meaningless at best, jingoist at worst. We have large swaths of people doing 'flaccid Agile,' a half-hearted attempt at following a select few software development practices, poorly… And worst of all, Agile methods themselves have not been Agile."*

We have come so far from the days of waterfall and yet we're still grappling with its hallmarks: wastage, failed products, software that doesn't solve problems, missed deadlines and blown budgets. Has anything actually changed in the last fifty years? It certainly doesn't look that way.

Working in the software development industry we, like countless others, quickly grew disillusioned with Agile and its many promises. The version of Agile being practised in most workplaces is really no more than a marketing gimmick, and an excuse for consultants to invent new buzzwords and spend inordinate amounts of money on coloured Post-it notes. It wasn't what we signed up for.

We recognised that in order to work effectively and build products that actually solve problems, we needed a new methodology; one that was in touch with the core principles of the Agile Manifesto in theory, but still easily applicable in practice. In particular, we wanted a methodology that:

1. Addressed the barriers to true agility, namely the way projects are chartered and funded;

2. Earnestly delivered on the true values of Agile and lean methodologies, such as customer centricity and iterative implementation;

3. Eliminated the seventy-five per cent of financial waste we see in projects today; and

4. Solved real problems for real people.

It took us a few years of trial and error, but we eventually developed a methodology that enabled us to achieve these goals, always in less time than it would take in an Agile project (and usually at a small fraction of the cost). In this chapter, we'll explain the methodology, it's key tenets and how we apply it to our projects at 3wks.

The methodology

If there's one thing we've learned throughout our careers, it's this: if we don't change how we look at problems and how we fund projects or break down implementation, then everything that follows is doomed to be "waterfrAgile." That's why we've developed the 3wks methodology and committed to life beyond Agile.

That isn't to say we've renounced Agile. The 3wks methodology is not designed to replace the Agile Manifesto or its twelve principles; we love both of those, and we stand on the shoulders of the giants who codified them. The 3wks methodology also adopts elements of extreme programming, Kanban and other lean methodologies (sometimes in their entirety) because we love those too. That's why we've devoted a whole chapter of this book to them (Chapter 4).

We reject Scrum, however, because it's wasteful marketing twaddle that breaks the first principle of the Agile Manifesto and contributes nothing to the others. In fact, it's fair to say that we hate what Scrum and what it has done to software development. You'll find a more detailed explanation of why we feel this way in Chapter 4.

What we've done at 3wks is codify some more concrete suggestions on how to actually deliver on the Agile Manifesto (without inheriting Scrum, which in many people's eyes is synonymous with Agile today). More specifically, we've recognised that the Manifesto and its principles need to be applied to the very early non-technical stages of problem investigation, before the business case is written and certainly well before a solution is invented by a non-practitioner working in an ivory tower.

Core tenets

Define the "contract" or "charter" in terms of business outcomes or benefits, not functional scope.
For funding and governance purposes.

Implement the solution gradually, from the center outwards, from the beginning of the project.
In order to achieve the WIP rule.

Work with users to understand their needs, not "the business";

Looking at challenges and projects this way, we've been able to isolate the core tenets of the 3wks methodology:

- Define our "contract" or "charter" in terms of business outcomes or benefits, not functional scope (for funding and governance purposes);

- Implement the solution gradually, right from the beginning of the project (in order to achieve the WIP rule);

- Work with users to understand their needs, not "the business";

Let's explore each tenet in isolation. The first is quite simple: in a project using the 3wks methodology, we commit to (or contract to) outcomes rather than a big, exhaustive scope document that typically takes three or four months to build. We don't commit to delivering a big list of features, priorities or an architecture. Instead, we define outcomes and commit to them.

This has a fundamental impact on project governance, but it's sometimes easier said than done. Identifying a set of outcomes to deliver without engaging in a protracted process of analysis (and falling victim to what we call 'analysis paralysis') can be a challenge. So what does an outcome actually look like? And how do we define it?

When identify outcomes with a group of stakeholders or users, there are four key things we try to define:

1. Problem(s)

2. User base

3. Success

4. Core capabilities

The first thing we try to define is the problem, and we ask ourselves and our stakeholders: what is the actual problem we're trying to solve?

Every project aims to solve problems, but what you'll find in most projects is that the discussion around a problem (or set of problems) morphs quickly into a discussion around possible solutions for that problem. All too often a conversation intended to isolate a problem ends up being an exploration of various off-the-shelf software products that could potentially solve it. The inability to fully understand or define a problem has been the key issue underlying some of the biggest project failures we've had to fix and fettle in our time.

So to define an outcome we try to understand which specific problem we're hoping to solve, and we avoid coming at that problem with a systems or solutions focus. It's imperative that we identify the number one problem to focus on during the project, and isolate that before moving on to find solutions.

Define to discover outcomes

Problems	**User-base**	**Success**	**Core capabilities**
What is the primary problem we're trying to solve?	When will we have access to users? And who are they?	What will success look like at the end of this project?	What 4-5 functional capabilities are needed to solve a problem and deliver an outcome?

Let's consider a simple example of this process in action. A client has gathered some customer feedback, perhaps through a Net Promoter Score survey, and finds that it needs to work on improving customer satisfaction. Customers are annoyed with certain processes, and there are too many people involved in the process internally. The business needs to make customers happier, but also reduce the amount of resources it allocates to certain processes.

Prior to commencing a project we'd investigate these problems - poor customer satisfaction and resource-intensive processes - and try to identify the one that should be our initial primary focus. This exercise quickly surfaces the primary driver of the project, and that gives us our starting point. We won't start a project if the client insists that two or more problems must remain primary (because it pulls the project apart at some point, usually between two sponsors).

The second thing we try to define when identifying outcomes is the user base. The 3wks methodology doesn't just pay lip service to customer centricity; everything we do, including the way we define and contract to outcomes, requires the input of users.

We won't start a project without knowing:

1. Which users we will pilot with and how this relates to the initial solution;

2. Details of the pilot users and how we will contact them on the first day; and

3. How we will expand from the pilot group to a successively broader base.

Understanding the user base isn't necessary to defining the outcomes themselves, but it is crucial in facilitating an incremental rollout (the primary failure of Agile in practice). It's important that we understand, across the board, why we're accessing users, who we are (and aren't) accessing, and when we'll be able to engage with them. Being able to engage users from day one is central to defining the requirements of the project, and to understanding what success looks like - more on that later.

A project won't start without knowing

Which users we will pilot with and how this relates to the initial solution.

Details of the pilot users and how we will contact them on the first day.

How we will expand from the pilot group to a successively broader base.

What we're trying to do here is acquire users for the project, and a key phrase we use here is 'first user first.' Having to amass a group of users can be a daunting premise for some project managers and organisations, so to actually get a cohort of users we can use, we conceptualise (and acquire) the user base in terms of incremental delivery.

It sounds complex, but it's not. We simply ask: who will be the first user to use the solution, and where are we getting them from? Who will be in the second group of users? Who will be in the third, fourth, or fifth? We may even ask who these people are, and what key attributes define them. Are they internal or external to the organisation? Are they technically-savvy or not?

We split the accessible user base, plus the successively more sophisticated solution, into broad implementation phases. This makes the task of user acquisition easier (because we can spread it out over time) and it keeps the focus on the most current group of users - in other words, the people who will receive and use the most recent iteration of the product. Instead of scrambling to find a big group of people to test the product on, we release to small groups of users incrementally and focus on the feedback we get from them. It's more manageable, and it's low risk.

Where do we find these people? Sometimes a client or sponsor will connect us directly to some preselected users. Other times, we'll walk around the building or even outside to find willing participants. It's not always easy. There are all sorts of potential blocks and organisational barriers that prevent us from directly communicating and collaborating with users. In the early days we found ourselves in situations where we'd been told that we'd be given access to users when a project commenced, only to find ourselves waiting three months passed before we met any of them.

Hence the golden rule of the 3wks methodology: when defining outcomes at the beginning of the process, understand and verify the user base up front. If possible connect with the pilot users before you start, and get confirmation that you'll have access to them from day one.

The third thing we try to do when defining outcomes supports the process of problem definition: defining what success looks like.

It's important that we're clear in both a rational and emotional sense about what a successful outcome will look like in a given project. Here, we're trying to paint a picture of the end of the pilot or the project and we ask ourselves: is this the end game? A crystal clear answer to that question is the goal.

Sometimes this is the part of the pre-project work that is the most difficult. This is especially true if you have a group of users or stakeholders who aren't experiencing much pain or for whom there is no gargantuan problem that needs to be solved. In this case, you can't settle. You have to work a little bit harder to tease out their vision of success, because this vision will be an important point of reference throughout the project.

Listening to people, asking questions, hypothesising about success and questioning the validity of that hypothesis is a good way to get people thinking about outcomes and picking the ones that resonate the most. A process like this should really only take an hour or so, but it's importance can't be overstated. Undertaking a project that doesn't have a clear end goal or picture of success is like running a marathon with no finish line. It's hard to know how far you've come, and the race may never end.

The last thing we try to define in the process of identify outcomes are the core capabilities. This is a synthesis of all our findings and insights gathered when we defined the problem, the user base and what success looks like.

The core capabilities looks like a simple list, and it's the closest thing in the 3wks methodology to a scope document. It's by no means detailed;

it simply talks to the high-level functions of the product being developed. It usually consists of around four or five bullet points that outline what capabilities need to be built into a product to solve a primary problem for a group of users.

To better illustrate this process, let's consider an example. A government Minister's office receives a fairly high volume of briefing papers, and it needs a product or solution to effectively manage the intake and processing of those papers. In exploring this problem, a few core capabilities emerge. The solution must allow users to:

- Author a briefing paper using a web page;

- Pass the paper from person to person electronically;

- Approve (or reject) the paper;

- Generate a PDF version of the paper for printing by the aide; and

- Track the history of each paper for audit purposes;

In just five bullet points, we've described the functional scope for a product in a project that will run from nine to twelve weeks and deliver an outcome (streamlining and simplifying the briefing paper submission process) for a group of users (the Minister's staff).

At the end of the day, this is a draft list that gets given to a project team. If they determine that there's a better way to achieve an outcome or solve a problem with a different list of core capabilities, then we'll change it. After all, we're all clear on what the real goal is, right?

So, to review: the core of the 3wks methodology is the notion of contracting to an outcome, not a mammoth scope document or feature list. But identifying that outcome isn't always straightforward, so we try to define four key things to arrive at an outcome we all agree on:

1. **The problem.** What is the primary problem we're trying to solve?

2. **The user base.** When will we have access to users? And who are they?

3. **The success factor.** What will success look like at the end of this project?

4. **The core capabilities.** What four or five functional capabilities do we need to build in order to solve a problem and deliver an outcome?

By now you will have realised that the 3wks methodology is all about incremental delivery; in fact, it's the second principle of the methodology. But unlike others, this methodology sees increments delivered nearly every week, beginning in week one. That's a much faster pace than you would typically see in a standard Agile or lean project.

If you've been involved in a software development project, even an Agile one, you'll know that there may be at least year's worth of work to do before you get funding for a project. A third of your time will then be spent doing some sort of high-level planning, where you'll build epic user stories or scope documents. Then you'll 'do some Agile' and commence a testing process at the end.

In reality, these are glorified waterfall projects - even if they're doing Agile in the middle. You're never actually releasing software to users from the beginning, or involving them in the development of a product being built for their benefit. And that's a fundamental issue.

Our mission is to build real products and software for users in the real world, and we do that by starting small at the beginning, releasing a build in the first week, and gradually ramping up towards the end. We keep users involved throughout the process, and we never go longer than three weeks without releasing an initial build to a user base.

You will have also noticed that the third principle of the 3wks methodology - user centricity - is at the heart of every process. What makes this methodology so novel (and so different from its lean and Agile counterparts) is that it gets requirements directly from the users, not from the business or the people who are commissioning the project.

Consider a 'traditional' project. Such a project typically consists of a project team, perhaps some business analysts, solution designers and technical architects. All of these people are talking to 'the business', whom we tend to think of as a single entity responsible for making decisions about features, budget and other important things. Herein lies the problem: that entity and that group of people are not the users of the product they're trying to build. They are not their own customers, trying to submit a briefing paper for review or research an insurance policy online. Often, those involved in representing the users, defining the requirements and signing them off are one, two or three steps removed from real users. The result? We have a project team operating with secondhand information, and the whole development exercise becomes a game of Chinese whispers.

This is why the 3wks methodology values user involvement and takes it to such an extreme. We don't start a project until a user base is defined because we need to be able to immerse the core project team into that user base from day one. Why? Because we work directly with those users to identify and unpack problems, core capabilities and more - things we can't afford to misunderstand or get lost in translation. We engage with users and ship product directly to them, and we spend ninety-nine per cent of our and budget actioning from those users.

As a result, that faceless business entity from earlier has a much lighter touch on the project. We don't rely on them for requirements or decisions because we've got a clear understanding of the outcomes, the problem and the core capabilities as defined by the people who matter most - the users.

Naturally, we don't just do everything the users want and action every piece of feedback we get. But we know that we have to keep users happy if we're going to achieve the outcome we've agreed with the business. In the grand scheme of things, working this way separates the need to make decisions around outcomes and priorities from the other job of sitting with users and understanding what really works for them. It makes for a more efficient project, and a more useful end product.

Scoping and costing a project

We've talked at length about delivering to outcomes, how we define those outcomes at the beginning of the process, and what impact this way of working has on our interactions with users and clients.

But what about its impact on the banalities of projects? How do we work out the duration or cost of a project if we're contracting to an outcome? How can we remain confident about our ability to deliver that outcome?

This is where breaking a problem into core capabilities becomes very important. Think back to the example of the Minister's office, and the process of submitting and reviewing a briefing paper. It would be quite easy to deliver a solution in a week that could meet the five bullet point capabilities that we identified earlier. It is, after all, just a webform.

When we start to define projects and problems in terms of core capabilities, we realise that a particular outcome can be delivered for $10,000 or $1,000,000. The difference between those deliveries isn't how much benefit they bring to the user. The difference is often in the design, or how well it works in a thousand small edge cases. In terms of actually meeting the core capabilities and delivering the agreed outcome, both options are perfectly valid.

The point is this: the 3wks methodology isn't about delivering slick, polished solutions in one week. That would barely be possible, and it would certainly be unsustainable. What we do instead is focus on building the core capabilities that can deliver for eighty per cent of the users, and eighty per cent of the use cases. You could call this a minimum viable product, or MVP. We just call it the 80/20 rule.

The logic behind this is simple too. Delivering the capabilities that meet the needs for eighty per cent of the users and edge cases means you're in the sweet spot, and getting the most 'bang for your buck.' As soon as you begin delivering beyond that eighty per cent, you've entered the territory of diminishing returns. In other words, you're delivering more than what is actually required to solve a problem.

Identifying core capabilities and aiming to meet that eighty per cent makes it easier to scope and estimate a project. We can ask ourselves, based on our experience, how long it would take us to build basic versions of the capabilities listed for a project. This is typically a quick, high-level discussion and takes less than an hour.

Based on that conversation, we can start talking timelines. We always talk in terms of weeks per team. We might say it will take four weeks to get to a MVP, and then we'll allow another four weeks to take us to the end of the project. It's a simple equation: we estimate how long it will take to build core capabilities, and then we double that estimate.

Doubling the estimate gives us a time-boxed budget for what we call 'enhancements.' Enhancements aren't strictly required in order to deliver the outcome, but in our experience clients are always happier with a second-generation MVP. When we begin a project, we have no idea what enhancements will be made after the core capabilities are delivered. It's a blank slate, and we don't contract to enhancements. An enhancement might be a slicker UX for a high-volume feature, a non-essential bug fix for a small group of users or a bit of spit and polish on branding.

The key thing to realise here is that the additional time budgeted for enhancements is finite, and we don't start building enhancements until we agree that the core capabilities have been delivered. There's a turning point in a project where we sit down and agree on whether or not the core capabilities have been delivered in MVP form, and only once we've reached consensus do we commence build on enhancements.

If there's a long list of enhancements - say, forty or more - we make it clear that we won't get them all done in the given timeframe. There's a finite amount of time to work with and we'll deliver enhancements one by one until we run out of time or money. Enhancements are delivered sequentially and we always focus first on the ones we collectively feel will make the biggest difference to the outcomes, or to the satisfaction of the user base. We don't set priorities; we just focus on the top few at any point in time. Remember that by this stage we've already delivered the core business benefits, and everything we're doing is an added bonus - one that comes at an extra cost. This is the arena of diminishing returns. Enhancements don't deliver much in terms of return on investment, but they are still each a matter of cost versus benefit.

If the project goes longer than six months we'll break it into phases, pull out the core capabilities and find a way to deliver them individually with some enhancements at the same time. It's like throwing a dinner party and serving several main courses with a side dish. It's still a fluid process, but it provides a lot of tactical governance.

Project governance and team structures

A traditional project typically has a dedicated project team consisting of a project manager and a few specialists - developers, testers, solution designers, etcetera - arranged in a hierarchical structure. These people form one group, and that group collectively reports into 'the business.'

That business represents a theoretical group of users. We say theoretical because, as we discussed earlier in this chapter, the people who represent the business and have authority over decision making typically have little to no exposure to their users and customers. This often results in a misrepresentation of user needs and requirements.

This hierarchical team model (where the project team reports to a project manager who, in turn, reports to 'the business') worked well in the 1970's when projects weren't as complex - more on that in Chapter 3. These were projects aimed at automating paper-based processes, or exploiting the limited capabilities of hardware.

Few projects meet that criteria today. Furthermore, the hierarchical team model falls apart as soon as you have to deal with users who are outside of your organisation. Why? Because the gulf between 'the business' and your users becomes insurmountably huge. There's a great deal of pressure on people in the business to make decisions that they're not comfortable (or capable of) making, because they don't have sufficient knowledge or interaction with users to do so. They end up assuming that every feature is critical, everything is important, and the product has to cover all bases. The result is scope creep, and a product that does everything but satisfies nobody.

This organisation model fails primarily because the number of communication lines between the project team, the business and users is too great. There are too many people talking to each other, and too many chefs in the kitchen. This creates a myriad of opportunities for misunderstanding - a risk that multiplies if you're also not documenting or writing down requirements.

Having experienced this sort of organisational model many times throughout our careers, we knew it wouldn't work for the 3wks methodology. We tried making it work, but it always broke down.

So we had to look elsewhere to find an organisational model and a way of structuring our teams that works with the methodology. After exploring a few different avenues, which we won't address here, we turned to nature and mathematics.

A fractal, in very basic terms, is a self-repeating, never-ending pattern. Fractals are infinitely complex, and they're created by the repetition of patterns usually at progressively smaller scales. They appear everywhere in nature - in snowflakes, trees, seashells, hurricanes - and they're a helpful concept for understanding how we can scale teams.

The first person to use the term 'fractal' was mathematician Benoit Mandelbrot in the 1970s, and he described fractals as 'beautiful, damn hard and increasingly useful.' His main focus then was on something called the 'theory of roughness' and he wanted to create a mathematical formula that could explain the formation of objects in nature.

But he also believed that fractals could explain more than natural phenomena. Nearly everything, he found, could be understood in terms of fractals. They can even be found in the creations of humans, in things like paintings and compositions. Fractals, Mandelbrot argues in *The Misbehaviour of Markets: A Fractal View of Risk, Ruin, and Reward*, are even a useful concept for analysing stock market volatility.

What Mandelbrot did in his illustrious career was take a mathematical concept and extends its scope and explanatory power beyond 'traditional' science. And that paved the way for people like Margaret Wheatley.

Wheatley, an influential management consultant, was the first to introduce the concept of a fractal organisation in her seminal book *Leadership and the New Science*, published in 1992. Life, Wheatley says, is a vast web of interconnections that demands cooperation and participation. The very best organisations, she says, have a fractal quality to them:

> *"Fractal organisations, though they may never have heard the word fractal, have learned to trust in natural organising phenomena."*

High functioning teams and organisations structure themselves in a pattern that enables greater communication. Instead of information trickling down a hierarchy from the top to the bottom, fractal organisations give everyone a role to place in the dissemination of information. The result is a much more efficient and collaborative team - and one that is able to scale as a project or business grows without breaking down.

Our goal was to develop an organisational model that didn't involve a top-down approach in which a group of people reported to another group of people who, in turn, reported to yet another group of people. What we came up with was something very much inspired by fractals, and by the work of Mandelbrot and Wheatley.

Our teams look like this: we have a core nucleus consisting of three people, usually one consultant and two developers. This core nucleus reports to the client's business engagement lead - the person who feels the pain from today's "problem." This is the person who will be making decisions in the project - and they're involved in all of the key discussions, in a light-touch way.

A classic 3wks team structure

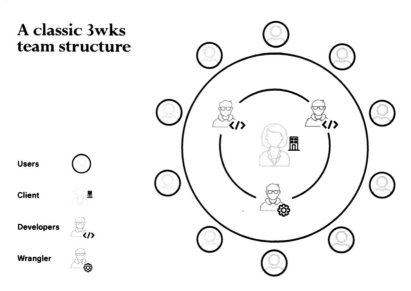

Users

Client

Developers

Wrangler

The figure above illustrates this structure in practice. You'll see that every member of the core nucleus is connected to a single engagement lead, and they're surrounded by users. The circle encompassing the core team is like a permeable cell membrane: information travels through it in both directions, with information from users flowing directly in while decisions and products flow out. There is no filtering of information from users via another person or team.

There is also no hierarchy. The structure is inherently flat. Instead of controlling the flow of information and decision making from the top down, this structure immerses the project team in the user base and facilitates activities that are fundamental to the 3wks methodology. It also isolates the client and the business. In this model, the client is relegated to an inner position and is not the conduit through which information from users flow. Their primary role is to make decisions internally, to agree on outcomes, approve core capabilities, etcetera.

If a project requires additional resources, they're organised behind one of the three individuals in the core nucleus. An additional two developers, for example, will report to a developer in the core nucleus. They too have direct access to users. The result is a self-repeating pattern, a team structure that is (in theory) infinitely scalable and always connected to the user base.

An expanded team structure

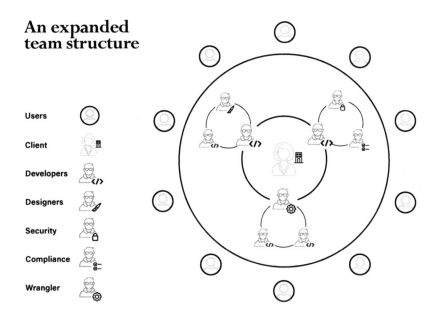

Users

Client

Developers

Designers

Security

Compliance

Wrangler

Working this way, among many other things, allows us to maintain fractal pattern integrity. Simply put, it's a structure that enables two-way communication between team members, engagement leads and users. It's an organisational model that puts the team directly in communication with the user base, and isolates decision making internally.

When does the 3wks method work best?

It's difficult to find a methodology to suit all situations, and we don't claim to have done that. Before you apply the 3wks methodology to your own organisation, we recommend assessing its suitability.

We can postulate, based on the 190 projects we've run so far, that projects well-suited for the 3wks methodology are those where there is:

1. An urgent and large commercial imperative with senior buy-in;

2. A human-centric problem with a large group of users;

3. A way to measure success, either in quantitative or emotional terms; and

4. Autonomy to define or redefine the solution to achieve the outcome.

The methodology is specifically designed to solve problems, in particular those that relate to a business process or way of working. These are what we call human-centric problems; in other words, they're not implementation problems or execution problems. A piece of legacy software that no longer meets business needs is not a human-centric problem. A process that doesn't allow Ministry staff to review, circulate and approve briefing papers is.

When does 3wks work best

An urgent and large commercial imperative with senior buy-in;

A human-centric problem with a large group of users;

A way to measure success, either in quantitative or emotional terms;

Autonomy to define or redefine the solution to achieve the outcome;

So the methodology works best when it can solve a particular set of problems, but it also requires a clear outcome. That is, it works best in situations where we're able to articulate an ideal outcome, and where there is a focused vision of what we're trying to achieve.

And this brings us to yet another requirement. The 3wks methodology works best when the specifics of a project are yet to be determined. We're no longer in the age where we can engineer a solution to a problem based on the way people currently work or behave. Performing current state analysis (instead of future state analysis) was well suited to business environments in which technology was simply automating existing processes, and where there was a high degree of continuity in processes and in organisations themselves.

Things have changed. Since then, new business models and new products have disrupted the business ecosystem and created a paradigm shift.

It is not possible to create a good product or a good solution to a problem based solely on an understanding of the current state of play. The specifics of a solution should emerge through interactions with users and through iterations of the build. It's not possible to know everything up front.

Combining the first and second criterion in the above list, we can say that the methodology works best when the project is trying to achieve transformative change.

It's easy to think that the methodology is best suited to small, ad-hoc, low-risk projects because it breaks everything - processes, teams, the user base - into small fragments. But really, the methodology is most suited to big, well-funded projects that may run for twelve to twenty-four months. These are projects that are traditionally hard to conceptualise as smaller 'bits', but the 3wks methodology is designed to take these big projects and break them down. The team structure, the defining of outcomes and the focus on core capabilities makes it easy to deliver big, transformative pieces of work - often at a fraction of the expected cost or time. This is where the value of the methodology really becomes evident.

But it doesn't work for every case. The 3wks methodology is not suited for projects where:

1.   The solution has already been determined;

2.   Package software is perceived to solve the business problem;

3.   The organisation has convinced itself that "big bang" is the only way, or:

4.   There is a general aversion to all things new and different.

As we said before, the methodology is specifically designed to solve human-centric problems. It's not designed for projects where the core of an identified problem is an existing solution that's been poorly implemented, or where the solution to a problem has already been identified (often as a piece of off-the-shelf enterprise software). If you, for example, have identified the need to improve information-sharing in your organisation and decided an intranet is the best solution for that problem, then the 3wks methodology is probably not for you.

The methodology is also not designed for 'big bang' projects. These are projects where development continues for years, and then a build is released to to user base all at once. If, for whatever reason, this is how you'd like to run a development project, then the 3wks methodology isn't a good fit for it. It's designed to do the exact opposite.

The 3wks methodology is also not a good fit if there is no one in the project team or the organisation who buys into it. The success of the methodology, like many others, depends on your commitment to upholding it. Following the 3wks processes and implementing the team structure won't work if you're not committed to communicating with directly with users or releasing builds incrementally.

A final thought: the suitability of the 3wks method doesn't just depend on what kind of project and problem we're dealing with. There's also a question of when.

If you consider the traditional project lifecycle, there are two phases: the analysis and approval phase, and the implementation phase. The former is where the problem is identified, a business case is developed, and funding for the project is sought. This can take a lot of time, work and resources, and the result is normally a huge scope document that is then given to the IT department (who have probably only just learned of the project's existence) for implementation.

The 3wks methodology works best when it's followed from the beginning, in the analysis and approval stage. Why? Because it makes it easier to define outcomes, develop a list of core capabilities and agree on deliverables up front, at the beginning of the project, than to work back from an existing scope or list of requirements. We want to create the oil painting ourselves, not strip back or paint over its layers and start again.

Moving beyond Agile

If we're being honest, the 3wks methodology isn't earth-shatteringly original or groundbreaking. It's a true melange of different existing methodologies, frameworks and ideas, and it pays homage to the Agile and lean practices that came before it.

But what is different about the 3wks methodology is its commitment to delivering real, usable software that solves actual problems for real users. Not to be platitudinous, we know that this methodology is critical for pulling off large-scale transformations and building products that people use. Agile is dead, and the new era of software development needs to go beyond its mangled principles and practices. It's time to go beyond Agile, and this is how we're doing it:

1. We contract to outcomes;

2. We ship product incrementally from the get-go;

3. We get requirements from the users;

4. We organise ourselves using a fractal organisational model that immerses teams within the user base; and

5. We say what we're going to deliver, and we deliver it.

Simple, really.

How we go beyond agile

Contract to outcomes   Ship product incrementally from the get-go   Get requirements from the users   Organise ourselves using a fractal organisational model that immerses teams within the user base   Say what we're going to deliver, and we deliver it.

A Dance in the Dark Every Monday

George Santayana, whom the *Stanford Encyclopaedia of Philosophy* refers to as a 'principal figure in Classical American Philosophy', once said that those who do not learn history are are doomed to repeat it.

He wrote that in *The Life of Reason*, a five-volume tome published between 1905 and 1906 dedicated to the expression of his own moral philosophy. For decades after that other notable thinkers, leaders and writers echoed Santayana's sentiment like a broken record. History, it seems, is as essential for our understanding of the present as it is for the past.

And so as we recount our story and explore new, evolving ways of working and developing software, it makes sense to look back at the past and the methodologies that have come before us. After all, they have shaped our current thinking and influenced how we work.

For many of us, the contents of this chapter is familiar and rather rudimentary. But it covers some key concepts and methodologies that are, for all intents and purposes, rather basal. Understanding how, when and why they were used is helpful for understanding our present. History is the example and instructor of the present, or so said Cervantes. So let's begin.

Waterfall

The concept of a 'software development methodology' originated in the 1960s with the emergence of the systems development life cycle (SDLC). The SDLC isn't a methodology per se; it's really more of a spectrum of methodologies made up of a few basic models, which we'll delve into later.

At its most basic, SDLC is about structure. It provides a sequential set of activities for designers and developers to follow, encapsulated in a set of steps or 'phases.' These phases - often called planning, analysis, design and implementation - are essential to the SDLC method and strictly adhered to as a matter of course.

Why, you ask? Because together they form an actionable (and predictable) model for creating functional systems in large scale, corporate projects. When SDLC was emerging, IBM was renting hard disk drive space to companies for a cool $3, 200 per month (that's about $26,388 in today's money) and agility was a risk exposure, not a priority. The stakes were high, computational power came at a premium and project failure was simply not an option.

The SDLC made sense for its time, and it paved the way for some of the most well-known and widely practiced software development methodologies of the 20th century. One of these methodologies is waterfall.

In the tradition of the SDLC, waterfall is a sequential design and development process. Its creation is often attributed to Winston Walker Royce, a pioneering American computer scientist, but the real accolades perhaps belong to Herbert Benington who was using the method (or at least his version of it) at MIT's Lincoln Laboratory in the mid-1950s. Attributions aside, the term 'waterfall' didn't even emerge until the 1970s at least, and Royce's 1970 paper *Managing the Development of Large Software Systems* is the methodology's de facto magna carta.

In the paper Royce describes a method of working that is grounded in analysis, program design, documentation and process. A *lot of* process. That process looks a bit like this:

1. System requirements gathering

This is the first step, and it's all about identifying, selecting and documenting the requirements of a project. Analysts and project managers typically work to create a briefing document that defines the project requirements in consultation with various stakeholders - a group that almost never includes end users or customers.

Here the project manager(s) may also estimate how much a project will cost, evaluate how much time it will take to complete, and complete a business case to justify the expense in front of senior management.

2. Software requirements gathering

This is the part where the software features needed to satisfy the system requirements are identified, selected and documented. At this point the software team will start working on the architecture, and they'll produce architecture documentation that outlines 'a solution' that, in theory, meets all the requirements of the project.

3. Analysis

Here the software requirements, features and proposed architecture are analysed against the requirements of the project, as well as constraints such as timing and funding. The architecture may need to be reworked, and things like budgets and timelines are revised.

4. Programme design

Now the fun part finally starts. In the fourth step, the bones of the software are mapped out and planned according to the objectives identified in the earlier steps. The design team starts working on the visual identity of the product and begins producing functional wireframes and a style guide. There might be some usability testing and a design review.

It's at this stage that a statement of work (SOW) is usually produced. This outlines what development work needs to be done, who is doing that work, and what that will cost. This is especially common for projects that require the services of an external or outsourced development team.

5. Development

The designed programme from step four finally goes into development, and coding begins.

6. Testing and quality assurance

Once the code is written and delivered, the project advances into the testing and quality assurance phase. Here the software is tested against the requirements outlined way back in steps one and two. Tests can include things like unit testing, integration testing and system testing. There is, naturally, a lot of recording and documenting of test cases and test results.

7. Delivery

Assuming the architecture, design and finished product meet the original requirements of the project, the software is finally delivered. This includes presenting, installing and configuring it for the intended user. Sometimes, resources are dedicated to supporting users post-delivery to troubleshoot any issues and bugs. *Fin.*

This is a very simplified version of waterfall, and it's also just that - a version. Waterfall exists in many different forms. But at the heart of the method is the notion of sequence; of arpeggiated steps, strictly followed. Progression to one step in the sequence is contingent on one's completion of its predecessor. There is no iteration. Once the water has flowed over the edge, the only way is down.

Waterfall is somewhat of a cumbersome methodology, but it's easy to see what made it so attractive in the late 20th century. By its very nature and design, waterfall enforced structure on development projects. It controlled decision-making processes and kept things moving along a predictable, manageable schedule of work that advanced from planning through to development. On paper it makes near-perfect sense.

This is perhaps why waterfall rose to great popularity in the first place, and why it remains the default *modus operandi* in many industries today. Automobile manufacturing is a good example of such an industry. When producing cars, manufacturers typically don't consult their customers at every step for their feedback. Why? Well, for the most part, car manufacturing is a heavily automated, standardised and regulated process - and with good reason. Making small iterations to the design of a car in response to customer feedback would likely result in some seriously unsafe, ugly, unbefitting cars. And there already enough of those on the market.

We also see waterfall in airplane manufacturing, bridge building, skyscraper construction - any large-scale project where making requirements changes halfway through the build requires millions in additional investment. We also see it in government projects. Indeed, the US Department of Defence famously embraced waterfall in its Military Standard for Defence System Software Development (MIL-STD-2167), released in 1985.

The standard required all government software to be developed and delivered using a process mapped out in Royce's 1970 paper, effectively making waterfall the default methodology for software development in the

United States. Later on in the 1990s, the German government published its Development Standards for IT Systems and in it the *Vorgehensmodell* or 'V-model' was named a requirement for all government and defence-related software projects. The goal of this model? To minimise project risks, to provide guidance for project planning and to outline a standardised production process that guaranteed quality.

The V-model remains the standard for German government projects to this day, but the same can't be said for the United States. In fact, it didn't take long for the US Department of Defence to update its procurement standards and officially recommend a more iterative approach to software development. This is unsurprising given that, according to Dr Jeff Sutherland, an evaluation of $34 billion worth of Department of Defence projects showed that seventy-five per cent of projects were complete failures; not a single line of code was used. The current instruction (published in 2003) lists incremental development and an 'evolutionary approach' as requirements for software projects.

And so we begin charting waterfall's epic downfall. Waterfall might be appropriate for building a bridge, but it's a problematic methodology for software development (which is arguably more of a fluid, malleable process and product). It's estimated that eighty-six per cent of waterfall projects fail.

Sutherland, speaking to Jonathan Crowe of OpenView, recounts his analysis of the FBI Sentinel project, another US government waterfall project. This project aimed to create a case management system that could supplant both digital and paper-based processes with purely digital workflows for investigations, and it started in 2006 with a budget of over $400 million. But even after several years, nothing functional had been produced. Eventually the vendor was dismissed, new leadership was appointed and the project was given a new team and a new budget. Sutherland explains:

> *"It was such a critical project that the FBI brought in an Agile Chief Information Officer and Agile CTO. They set up 15 guys in the basement of the FBI building, and a year later, after $400 million had been wasted, they spent $30 million, and the project came in under budget."*

It's a famous example of a waterfall project gone bad, and there are many like it. Missed deadlines, blown-out budgets, feature failures and unusable software are the modern trademarks of waterfall projects. This is the reason why some of the technology industry's biggest names - like Microsoft, Google and Spotify - have denounced it.

And there's valid reasons for doing so. As we now know, it is impossible (and inadvisable) to constrain design and development to a single step or stage. Iterations are critical to creating something that is fundamentally usable and 'performant.'

Furthermore, introducing testing at the end of the development phase makes absolutely no sense. Leaving it to the last minute invariably results in the realisation that the product fails to satisfy all requirements and that a redesign is required - usually after all the project's budget has been spent on consultants, designers, developers and whatever else. The infamous train wreck that was healthcare.gov in the United States followed a classic waterfall model and as a result, after years of development, underwent just six days for testing before it went live. "Anybody in software development," says Sutherland "knows that is a total disaster."

And this highlights another one of waterfall's many problems: it makes a lot of assumptions. Specifically, the methodology assumes that requirements, specifications and designs translate effortlessly into actual products that can be developed. Ask any developer and they'll tell you that this is almost never the case. There is a difference between what is conceivable and what is possible.

Winston Royce knew all of this and more. He never actually endorsed waterfall as an effective methodology for software development. He believed in it as a concept but felt that when implemented, it "invited failure." It's a sad fact of history that Royce's seminal paper Managing the Development of Large Software Systems is attributed with popularising a methodology Royce himself didn't believe in. His preferred method - outlined in the later chapters of this book - was an incremental development process that relies heavily on prototyping.

Chaos

"Invention," Mary Wollstonecraft once wrote, "does not consist in creating out of void but out of chaos."

Chaos has been the subject of many great thinkers from backgrounds as diverse as literature, mathematics and economics. Chaos theory, a branch of mathematics that focuses on the behaviours of dynamical systems, has been particularly influential on disciplines such as biology, robotics and cryptography. And software.

The chaos model is another member of the SDLC family, purportedly inspired by chaos theory and an ancient Chinese game called Go. According to Mike Cohn, one of the masterminds behind Scrum, a professor named L.B.S. Raccoon (a bizarre *nom de plume*) wrote the earliest known papers on the model.

Raccoon had apparently observed that the prevailing software development methodologies of the time, such as waterfall, were good at solving project problems and ensuring order, but they weren't good at solving technical problems. There were 'more technical' methodologies adept at solving technical problems, but they weren't suitable for projects - especially big ones. The chaos model was an attempt to bridge this methodological gap.

The model finds its roots in chaos theory, and it conceptualises engineering problems and code as just one part of a much bigger picture. Utilising the concepts of chaos and fractals, Raccoon explains:

> *"We know that large programs consist of many lines of code and that large projects consist of the daily efforts made by individual developers. We know that the large scale and the small scale somehow relate to each other. Yet most models of software development seem to focus on one extreme or another, ignoring the role of developers.*
> *…Users, developers, and technologies form a continuum throughout software development. They all interact in a complex dance."*

The model put forward by Raccoon in the 1995 paper *The chaos model and the chaos cycle* bears resemblance to chaos theory in its assertion that software isn't made in a vacuum; it's created in a complex system. And once you recognise that you're operating within a complex system, you have to accept that the results of your endeavours may be unpredictable. Some things, if not most things, are beyond our control.

The chaos model, then, is all about suspending control of 'the big things' and instead focusing on the small, solvable things first. High-level architectural issues in a software development project can't be resolved without first resolving 'smaller' issues, right down to problems with individual lines of code.

And this brings us to the guiding principle of the chaos model: always resolve the most important issue first. An issue in this context is defined as an incomplete programming task, and an issue becomes important if it is big, urgent or robust. A big issue is one that disrupts functionality or prevents value from being delivered to users, while an urgent issue is one that will prevent other work being done until it's resolved. A 'robust' issue is one that can be tested when resolved.

Here we start to see some of the fundamental ideas and assumptions underpinning the chaos model:

1. Projects are, by nature, complicated and chaotic;

2. The best solution to a problem depends on the context of the problem, for issues are the products of their environment; and

3. A project is essentially made up of many interrelated problems, best approached sequentially by order of importance.

To understand how the chaos model works in practice, it's helpful to think about meteorologists predicting the weather. Weather systems are fundamentally chaotic, nonlinear and unpredictable, which makes the business of producing a weather forecast quite difficult. So how do they do it? Meteorologists start by looking at the weather patterns of the previous day and comparing them with current conditions. Then they look at observations nearby and collect data on things like temperature, pressure, wind speed and precipitation, looking for patterns and movements in the atmosphere. They start by observing the big movements first, and then focus in on smaller details using satellite and radar technologies. In short, they use the insights gleaned from these smaller details to form the basis of a forecast.

Software developers follow a similar process when they're working with the chaos model. When confronted with a challenge (like a bug fix, or some other technical problem) they start by looking at the project as a whole before drilling down into systems, modules, functions and individual lines of code. It's a strategy that breaks big problems down into smaller, bite-sized problems that can be solved in a linear manner. The result is an iterative development process that forces a more symbiotic relationship to exist between developers and project managers.

This is what really distinguishes the chaos model from other methodologies. While other methodologies make light work of managing technical implementations and bug fixes, they're not resilient enough to survive in dynamic environments impacted by a variety of exogenous factors, like customer requirements. That's why, in theory, these projects fail or get delayed.

But there are other points of contrast between the chaos model and other methodologies, waterfall in particular. In the chaos model, a software development project is perceived as something structurally similar to a pomegranate: a whole, solid fruit made up of hundreds of tiny arils. A project isn't just one task or product - it's the combination of many small, individual tasks, features and activities. Waterfall, by contrast, looks at a project as a singular entity that moves through a series of processes as one.

And that's another point of difference. In the waterfall world, projects are initiated, requirements are designed, the software is built to completion and then issues are fixed. With the chaos model, things are a bit different; individual lines of code are treated as separate and issues are fixed incrementally, as they arise, and not left to the end. The logic here is that each line of code is a building block for the final product, and you can't build a sturdy wall by ignoring broken or fragile bricks along the way.

The chaos model certainly has its merits, but it's arguably more of a conceptual framework than a full-blown methodology. Its value is not so much in its practices, but in its implications. If we examine the chaos model and adopt of the paradigm of 'project as pomegranate' we learn one critical thing: developers need more than just technical skills to be able to understand and respond to situations that arise in a project. They need soft skills and a good deal of business acumen too.

Code and fix

This brings us to yet another methodology that falls along the SDLC spectrum, next to waterfall and the chaos model. It's called the 'code and fix' model and on the surface, it looks like a close cousin of the chaos model.

The model is simple: coding begins when a project commences, and problems are fixed as they arise. A project is considered complete when all the features are built and everyone agrees there are no more problems to fix.

What makes the code and fix approach different to the chaos model is in the term 'project.' See, in the chaos model, projects are still mammoth beasts and all the usual processes of requirements gathering, feature design and testing are followed. In the code and fix paradigm, a project is less of programme of work and more of an idea. Development of a product can start when all of its features and requirements may not have been fully thought out; there's no planning, and everything is very ad-hoc.

There are a few obvious benefits to working this way. First of all, it's an easy model to get your head around. Secondly, it could be argued that it helps deliver projects on budget as it reduces management overheads and time spent on planning. That's the real advantage here. Code and fix relieves developers of the need to spend extensive amounts of time defining requirements, preparing scope documents and more. They can get started with a rough idea of the end product in their heads, and focus on turning that idea into something tangible.

Working this way can be really effective in situations where the timeline is short, and the product being built is quite straightforward (or, at the very least, not the foundation for something much more complex). Writing in the *Computer Science Handbook*, Allen Tucker explains that it can "effective for very limited proof-of-concept demonstrations or throwaway prototypes to help evolve requirements." The model can also be useful, he says, "in testing the feasibility of a certain approach before more serious development is pursued."

But the code and fix model has some serious drawbacks too. In abandoning virtually all forms of up-front planning and requirements gathering, it foregoes some critical processes and decisions about design, architecture and build. It's a fast way of working but the absence of prior planning and ongoing testing means that if you uncover major architectural problems halfway through the build, you'll likely have to write large sections of the code.

And therein lies the biggest problem of the code and fix model: it can lead to some very expensive problems. The amount of planning and preparation that happens in waterfall projects is excessive, but a little bit of planning never hurt anyone. At the very least, it saves them some money.

The spiral model

Introduced by Barry Boehm in his 1986 paper *A spiral model of software development and enhancement*, the spiral model was a popular alternative to waterfall and a key SDLC methodology. Its origins are arguably found in waterfall, namely in its limitations and failures. Think of it as software's veritable lotus growing in the mud.

Boehm conceded that waterfall worked well in projects where requirements were clearly understood, but on the whole he felt that it fell short. He explains:

> *"A primary source of difficulty with the waterfall model has been its emphasis on fully elaborated documents as completion criteria for early requirements and design phases.*
>
> *For some classes of software, such as compilers or secure operating systems, this is the most effective way to proceed. However, it does not work well for many classes of software, particularly interactive end-user applications.*
>
> *Document-driven standards have pushed many projects to write elaborate specifications of poorly understood user interfaces and decision support functions, followed by the design and development of large quantities of unusable code."*

Waterfall's biggest problem, from Boehm's perspective, was that it didn't deliver well on its promise of usable software. It underestimates the complexity of projects and provides no mechanism for managing that complexity, or the inherent risk associated with complexity. So he developed the spiral model.

The spiral model, Boehm wrote, took years to evolve and is "based on experience with various refinements of the waterfall model as applied to large government software projects." At its core it's a risk-driven approach to software development that acknowledges the complexity of projects, much in the same way as the chaos model. Software projects, Boehm argued, are often at the mercy of risks and challenges such as cost overruns, changed requirements and loss of personnel or resources. The essential goal of the spiral model, therefore, is to minimise risks through prototyping and user feedback.

To understand how the model works, imagine a simple two-dimensional spiral. This spiral represents one cycle or 'sprint' in the development process, and it begins with identification of:

- the objectives of the aspect or feature of the product being built (such as functionality or performance);

- the alternative means of implementing this part of the product; and

- the constraints (such as cost or timing) preventing the implementation of those alternatives.

As the spiral radiates outward, the process moves on from identification and on to evaluation. Here, we identify areas of uncertainty and risk. There may be some uncertainty, for example, about the ability of certain features and functionalities in the product to meet the identified objectives. If that's the case, the next step is to formulate an effective low-cost strategy for resolving the risk. "This," Boehm writes "may involve prototyping, simulation, benchmarking, reference checking, administering user questionnaires, analytic modelling, or combinations of these."

If a prototype is robust and operationally useful, it serves as a low-risk base for the evolution of the product. The spiral continues as before, following the six basic steps: determine objectives, alternatives and constraints; identify and resolve risks; explore alternatives; produce deliverable; plan for the next iteration.

The entire point of the model is to reduce risk in phases and tackle the big problems early, asking questions like:

- Are we building the right product?

- Is this what our customers or users want?

- Can we build this product using existing technology?

This is probably what made it so initially attractive. In practice, the spiral model works by building progressively more 'complete' versions of the software by starting with a simple prototype and building on it, giving developers clarity and control right from the beginning of the project. With each loop of the spiral, customers evaluate prototypes and modifications are made to it accordingly. This is an important feature of the model, according to Boehm:

"An important feature of the spiral model, as with most other models, is that each cycle is completed by a review involving the primary people or organisations concerned with the product.

This review covers all products developed during the previous cycle, including the plans for the next cycle and the resources required to carry them out. The review's major objective is to ensure that all concerned parties are mutually committed to the approach for the next phase."

The spiral model is iterative and prototype-driven - something Winston Royce would have appreciated - but applying it to a project is slightly more complicated than you'd expect. It's handling of post-delivery maintenance and enhancement is lacking, and (as Boehm acknowledged in his paper) it seems to leave a lot of questions unanswered. How does one get off the spiral, for example? When does it stop spiralling?

Boehm's answers to these questions and his advice for applying the spiral model is ironically dense given his criticism of waterfall and its detrimental reliance on "fully elaborated documents." But in an effort to further clarify the application and use of the model, he explores a case in which it was used.

TRW Defense Systems Group, part of TRW Inc (an American aerospace and automotive corporation that was once a pioneer in fields including software and systems engineering), had used the spiral model in the development of its Software Productivity System, an integrated software engineering environment.

The initial drive of the project was to improve productivity in key corporate operations, and software engineering was identified as one of those operations. The first circuit of the spiral involved a feasibility study, where the objective of increasing software productivity was critically evaluated. Then the spiral advanced to subsequent circuits that required further analysis, top-level requirements specification and prototyping. In the end, the Software Productivity System was successfully developed and eventually grew to support over three hundred tools and more than one million instructions. According to Boehm, all of the projects utilising the system increased their productivity by at least fifty per cent.

The primary advantage of the spiral model, Boehm believed, was that it retained a lot of the 'good features' of existing software development methodologies like waterfall, but avoided their pitfalls with its risk-driven approach. It's like waterfall, but better.

Not much better, though. Unfortunately the spiral model was really only suited to low-risk projects with stable requirements. And while it does a good job of bringing users into the process and encouraging iterative development, it's a very complicated, almost torturous model that requires diligent management. Boehm himself couldn't describe it without resorting to an array of diagrams, tables, lists and lengthy paragraphs. The paper where he outlines the model is no less than twenty five pages long.

Rapid Application Development

Another iterative methodology in the SDLC tradition is James Martin's Rapid Application Development (RAD) model.

Rapid Application Development is a term often used to describe SDLC methodologies more broadly, but Martin's model (introduced in the 1991 book *Rapid Application Development*) is in a league of its own.

The model is often positioned as the polar opposite to waterfall, emphasising rapid prototyping and iterative delivery. Much like the spiral model, the RAD model shuns waterfall-style planning and instead seeks to produce working software in less time. A RAD project typically follows four steps:

- **Requirements planning**. Designers, developers and users (or clients) come together and agree on the project's scope and requirements. Discussions around resourcing, budgets and timelines happen here.

- **User design**. Early prototypes are developed following interactive sessions with users, whose feedback is used to determine system architecture. This step is repeated as the project evolves.

- **Construction**. When basic user and system design has begun, the bulk of the coding, testing and integration work commences. Input from users is integrated constantly to further develop the product.

- **Cutover**. The final cutover or 'transition' stage (called 'implementation in waterfall') is where the development team moves components into a live production environment were testing or training can take place.

Like the spiral model, the RAD approach works well in situations where highly-skilled teams are put to task on a relatively low-risk project. RAD is effective in situations where time and money are limited, and where access to users (and their feedback) is easy. Unfortunately, also like the spiral model, RAD doesn't scale well to big projects with big teams. And while it's resilient enough to cope with changing requirements, it doesn't fare well in long-term, complex projects which may face all sorts of volatility.

The lifecycle models

It may seem that the methodologies explored thus far have little in common. Waterfall, for example, seems miles away from chaos or code and fix models. Likewise for the unfortunately convoluted spiral model.

But actually, all of these models share one common characteristic. They're lifecycle models, meaning they follow the traditional SDLC sequence: requirements gathering, design, implementation, testing, and maintenance.

Even the chaos and code and fix models, which forego any formal requirements gathering or design process, are lifecycle models. Why? Because in those models, testing and maintenance still follow on from implementation; never before, and never during.

There are, as we've seen, some enticing benefits to be had with these models. For one thing, they provide a clear and arguably intuitive work structure. They also force a consistent focus on the 'big picture' and that, in theory, helps projects move along to completion. But there are many more reasons why they were so popular among the software community in the late twentieth century:

- They help developers cope with unpredictable, dynamic environments subject to ever-changing requirements;

- They're appealing for people who have a lower tolerance for ambiguity; and

- They give people in organisations the stability they so desperately crave.

The SDLC models are still used today, but they emerged at a time much different to our own. Between the 1960s and 1980s, developers were grappling with a so-called 'software crisis,' a term coined by attendees of the 1968 NATO Software Engineering Conference in Germany. During that time, writing useful and efficient software programmes was extremely difficult because computers were rapidly advancing in computational power, increasing the complexity of the software required to run (and take advantage of) them. Edsger S. Dijkstra, an early pioneer in the field of computer science, reflected on these difficult times in his 1972 ACM Turing Lecture, *The Humble Programmer*:

> *"To put it quite bluntly: as long as there were no machines, programming was no problem at all; when we had a few weak computers, programming became a mild problem, and now we have gigantic computers, programming had become an equally gigantic problem.*
>
> *In this sense the electronic industry has not solved a single problem, it has only created them, it has created the problem of using its products. To put it in another way: as the power of available machines grew by a factor of more than a thousand, society's ambition to apply these machines grew in proportion, and it was the poor programmer who found his job in this exploded field of tension between ends and means."*

Programmers in the late twentieth century had found themselves between a rock and a hard place. It's no wonder, then, that the software development life cycle models took off. They provided structure, process and clarity. They didn't always work, but they made the seemingly insurmountable task of software development feel a whole lot more *doable*.

The problem is that these models, Tucker explains, can't cope with "the human dynamics of our users' perspectives." The software community, in a bid to shield itself from the tangled mess of society's ambitions and desires, had defaulted to a "problem first, people second" approach that fundamentally excluded users.

The community survived for many years in this comfortable realm, but the dawn of the new millennium changed everything. According to data collected by the International Telecommunications Union, specialised agency of the United Nations, the percentage of the world's individuals using the internet in the 1980s was close to zero. By 1995 that figure had risen to nearly one per cent. In 2000, nearly seven per cent of the world's individuals were using the internet; in the United States alone that figure was much higher - forty-three per cent.

Before then, the creation of 'digital' products and software was reserved for the software engineering elite. But in the 1990s it became much more possible for individuals to partake in the process. You could create and host your own content on GeoCities, or build a website with Tripod's groundbreaking (and unwieldy) WYSIWYG editor. Software's development lifecycle had shortened, and it was becoming easier (and more important) to build and deliver products faster.

And this is where the SDLC models started to erode; they weren't equipped for the new millennium. Waterfall and its counterpart methodologies were criticised for their complexity and their excessive overheads. They were too process-laden, and under their mandate it would take eons to build and deliver a piece of software.

So in the late 1990s we witnessed the emergence of 'lightweight' methodologies, like extreme programming. These methodologies were a shining beacon in the software community, a symbol of things to come. Agile, the hero among these new ideas and ways of working, was particularly groundbreaking.

Indeed, many say that the arrival of Agile in the 2000s began a new (and ongoing) era in software development, characterised by smart decision making and effective process. It's making us smarter, more productive, more in-touch with our end users. It's the hero we deserve, and the hero we need right now; it's our a silent guardian and watchful protector. There's just one problem with this theory:

Agile is already dead.

The rise and fall of 'lightweight' methodologies

In February 2001, seventeen people gathered at a ski resort in the Wasatch Mountains of Utah. Among them they shared an impressive list of credentials: there were CEOs, scientists, rockstar programmers and software professionals innovating at the edge of their field. Together they hoped to do one thing: find common ground. Oh, and ski.

This self-described 'gathering of organisational anarchists' spent two days talking, arguing and pontificating about the virtues and problems of software development. It wasn't the first time they had met. Many of them were colleagues (or competitors) and the subject of their intense three-day conversation - 'light' programming methodologies - had also been the focus of several earlier gatherings.

Kent Beck, an American software engineer and creator of the 'extreme programming' (XP) methodology, had organised a meeting the spring before the gathering in the Wasatch Mountains took place. It was there that a few proponents of XP and some sanctioned outsiders first vocalised communal support for 'light' methodologies. Nothing formal came of the meeting, however, save for a few articles published in the year after about 'light' and 'lightweight' processes.

And then Bob Martin, prolific author and software engineer, floated the idea of convening a small conference to 'get all the lightweight method leaders in one room.' And so the trip to Utah was organised, and the Agile Manifesto was born.

The Agile Manifesto is undoubtedly one of the most important 'documents' in the history of software. Its contents is brief. In fact, it consists of just four core values:

- Individuals and interactions over processes and tools
- Working software over comprehensive documentation
- Customer collaboration over contract negotiation
- Responding to change over following a plan

The fact that such a diverse (and highly opinionated) group of software professionals managed to write such a concise, insightful piece of prose is amazing. The twelve guiding principles they drafted (which support the values) are also forthright and deeply discerning. Indeed, the entire manifesto reads more like the work of Rumi than your average professional document, much less one written by engineers likely more familiar with hexadecimal code strings than poetry. The Agile Manifesto is a thing of beauty, no doubt. But, to quote Donna Tartt, *beauty is terror.*

When it came out, the Agile Manifesto was to software what Julia Child was to french cuisine: accessible, sophisticated and a breath of fresh air. But in spite of its accessibility and the pedigree of its authors, just about every one of the values in the Agile Manifesto has been ignored or hideously distorted by the software development community. With a few notable exceptions, Agile values have been sacrificed at the altar of change-averse enterprise IT departments. Why? Because the values are intellectually and emotionally challenging, and change is different.

The authors of the manifesto knew this would happen. Writing about its history, they explained:

"In order to succeed in the new economy, to move aggressively into the era of e-business, e-commerce, and the web, companies have to rid themselves of their Dilbert manifestations of make-work and arcane policies.

This freedom from the inanities of corporate life attracts proponents of Agile Methodologies, and scares the begeebers (you can't use the word 'shit' in a professional paper) out of traditionalists. Quite frankly, the Agile approaches scare corporate bureaucrats— at least those that are happy pushing process for process' sake versus trying to do the best for the "customer" and deliver something timely and tangible and "as promised"—because they run out of places to hide."

The values and principles spelled out the Agile Manifesto are arguably just common sense. They're not enigmatic or wrapped in deeper meaning.

But what they are in the corporate world is heresy; they challenge the status quo and subvert the dominant paradigm of survival of the procedural. At face value they appear to go against the collective interests of those who build, maintain and managing legacy systems. They're a threat to anyone who is trying to hold on to their seat.

As a result of this, we've seen Agile's grotesque bastard children rear their ugly heads in organisations far and wide. We've seen software professionals carry on with requirements gathering and redundant processes, eschewing the value of human interactions, working software, collaboration and resilience, all while proudly waving the Agile flag. We've seen project teams buried deep in business cases and compliance manuals, waiting for the day they can start coding. We've seen end users cast out into the cold in favour of business analysts who speak for everyone, controlled by project managers who rule by scope.

It's at this point, sixteen years after the emergence of the Agile Manifesto, that we have to ask ourselves: what happened? How did we generate so much excitement for 'lightweight' development methodologies, only to screw it up? *How and why* is Agile dead?

In this chapter, we'll attempt to deal with these questions and continue the exploration into the history of software development methodology that we started in Chapter Three. This is as much a celebration of software's methodological pluralism as it is a eulogy for Agile. We'll start with a somewhat-brief foray into the world of 'light' methodologies - the ones that arguably formed the foundation of the Agile Manifesto - and then we'll tackle the big question of why Agile failed.

Extreme programming

Extreme programming (XP) came on to the software scene in the late 1990s. Developed by Kent Beck (but inspired and formulated by many others in the industry), XP was one of the earliest of the 'lightweight' methodologies to emerge. At its core, it was all about reconceptualising software development in the face of vague and changing requirements.

Speaking to German magazine *OBJEKTspektrum* in 2000, Beck described XP as "a step towards a new paradigm of software development." He explains:

"In the older paradigms, software was compared to existing activities, like mathematics, civil engineering, poetry, or electrical engineering. But software development is really fundamentally different than anything humans have done before, so any argument by analogy about how to do it is bound to limit its potential.

XP starts from the premise that programming is programming, but that you have to add some activities to sustain it over time- like testing and refactoring."

Described as a fundamentally 'humanistic' approach to software development based on the principles of simplicity, communication, feedback and courage, XP began to attract a lot of attention in the late 90s and early 2000s. Writing in his book *Extreme programming explained: embrace change* (which he wrote largely on a train between Zurich and Munich) Beck outlines the fundamental principles of XP:

- Distinguishing between the decisions to be made by business interests and those to be made by project stakeholders;

- Writing unit tests before programming and keeping all of the tests running at all times;

- Integrating and testing the whole system - several times a day;

- Producing all software in pairs;

- Starting projects with a simple design that constantly evolves to add needed flexibility and remove unneeded complexity;

- Putting a minimal system into production quickly and growing it in whatever directions prove most valuable;

- Don't force team members to specialise and become analysts, architects, programmers, testers and integrators - every XP programmer participates in all of these critical activities every day;

- Don't conduct complete up-front analysis and design - an XP project starts with a quick analysis of the entire system, and programmers make analysis and design decisions throughout;

- Develop infrastructure and frameworks as you develop applications, not up-front - delivering business value is the heartbeat that drives

XP projects; and

- Don't write and maintain implementation documentation - communication in XP occurs face-to-face.

That's a lengthy list of propositions for a methodology that disavows documentation, but it's an impressive one. Interestingly, it shares a number of insights and characteristics with SDLC models, namely the chaos model. Both XP and the chaos model, for example, correctly identify the importance of 'generalists' in software development. Too many specialists does not a good project make. XP also shares some common ground with Boehm's spiral model, namely in the fact that it encourages teams to put minimal systems into production quickly and iterate from there.

The rules and practices that make up the XP approach can be grouped into four categories: planning, designing, coding and testing. Coding, Beck says, is the heartbeat of XP; every aspect of a project's build goes under intense scrutiny many times throughout one day, and programmers continually develop and executive tests to make sure that what they've built is resilient. This is, perhaps, where the methodology get its name.

From a distance, XP is all about *short cycles, small releases and actioning concrete feedback*. Its techniques are designed to produce high-quality software in a way that is efficient and resilient in the face of changing requirements. It keeps the cost of change stable, and makes it possible to deliver a software programme that people will actually use. It's a development methodology for the business world.

Obviously, for XP to work, it needs a few things. One is a team of developers who are comfortable with (and capable of) wearing many hats and talking to customers to gather their feedback. The second thing, then, is customers. Customer feedback is crucial to the XP methodology and essential for building functional software. Customers need to be made available to the development team, and that development team must be motivated and eager to respond to those customers.

Extreme programming, however, does have a few disadvantages. Chief among those disadvantages is the sheer amount of attention and weight it puts on coding and the people who do the coding - programmers. Addressing the audience at the Fifth Annual Lean IT Summit in 2015, Beck reflected on XP and its underlying premise of 'programmers are priority.' The first edition of *Extreme programming* explained, he said, wasn't as inclusive as it should have been. The version of XP it described was programmer-centric, and to borrow Beck's words, it was 'snotty and disrespectful' towards the other people in development projects.

"Shockingly," Beck admits "that alienated a large number of people."

"Most people who write cheques, actually, get alienated when you tell them their job is redundant."

There was a huge surge of interest in extreme programming after it first emerged. But as is the case with most good ideas, interest in it gradually waned over time, perhaps because huge parts of it were alienating.

So for twenty years Beck set about making XP more inclusive, focusing on two key questions: who needs to be involved to create value-add software, and how can they be involved in a valuable way? We haven't yet seen good answers to these questions from Beck or anyone else in the software community. But taking development all the way to the customer and focussing on 'cycles of learning for everybody,' Beck says, would be a step in the right direction.

Crystal Clear

Some ten or so years after Beck published *Extreme programming explained*, Alistair Cockburn published *Joel on Software*

Cockburn, one of Beck's contemporaries and a fellow Agile Manifesto signatory, describes Crystal as a 'family' of methodologies based on a 'genetic code.' As with geological crystals, each Crystal methodology has a different colour that corresponds to project size and 'criticality.' Cockburn intentionally developed Crystal as a family of methodologies as opposed to a single, overarching methodology to solve the inherent challenges of methodology design: communication, scope and applicability. Each Crystal methodology, Cockburn says, isn't a 'kit of parts' to be followed, but a set of "samples that you adjust to your circumstances."

We won't take the time here to explore all of the various Crystal methodologies in turn; we don't have the time nor the patience. Instead we'll focus on the one that receives the most attention: Crystal Clear.

"Crystal Clear," Cockburn writes "is a highly optimised way to use a small, collocated team, prioritising for safety in delivering a satisfactory outcome, efficiency in development, and habitability of the working conventions."

A typical Crystal Clear team consists of a lead designer and two to seven developers, placed together in a large room equipped with "whiteboards and flip charts" where they can work free from distractions and with "easy access to expert users." The idea is that this team delivers running, usable code to users every month or two, and they adjust their working conventions periodically.

All Crystal methodologies focus on three core properties: frequent delivery, close communications and reflective improvement. "Crystal Clear," Cockburn explains "takes advantage of small team size and proximity to strengthen close communication into the more powerful osmotic communication." The Crystal Clear methodology is further characterised, he says, by its sense of personal safety, focus, easy access to expert users and strong technical environment. It's a methodology that empowers developers and encourages them to interact directly with users, speak their minds and focus on creating usable software.

There are a few great things about Cockburn's Crystal methodologies (their eccentric names not being one of them). The emphasis on small teams and easy access to users, for example, is commendable. Cockburn correctly recognised that frequently deploying working software to small user groups, or even just one friendly user, is critical for developing good products. This is something that we've put at the heart of the 3wks methodology, expanded in the earlier chapters of this book.

But Crystal Clear has a number of drawbacks as well. We don't think that releasing software every month or two really counts as 'frequent delivery,' and the methodology seems to place a lot of importance or value on rather arbitrary things like working environments. There are some important insights to be gleaned from the Crystal Clear methodology, but it largely falls short.

Feature-driven development

Another member of the lightweight methodology team is the feature-driven development (FDD) approach, initially developed by well-known author and IT strategist, Jeff de Luca.

Like XP and the Crystal methodologies, FDD "understands, embraces, and accepts software construction as a human activity." What makes FDD different from other lightweight methodologies, however, is that it values design above all else. It does not subscribe to the notion that design emerges through code, or vice versa. The unit of development in an FDD project, therefore, is a feature - not a line of code - and features (which de Luca describes as 'tiny, granular pieces of client-valued function) are completed every week.

A typical FDD project follows a few steps, which look something like this:

1. Develop an overall model. The project team outlines a high-level scope, understands initial requirements and attempts to establish some vision of the programme's architecture. This process can take days, and it doesn't include any feature definition.

2. Build a features list. This is where the team identifies features and estimates the time it will take to complete them. A feature that will take more than two weeks to build is 'decomposed' into sub-features; most features take much less than two weeks to build. At this point features are not weighted or prioritised, because doing so at this stage is too labour intensive and time consuming, and it adds little value to the process.

3. Plan by feature. Here the features are put into a sequence based not on qualifiers such as 'must have' or 'nice to have', but with consideration of business activities and external milestones such as pilots, betas, feedback sessions, previews and so on. This preserves the integrity of the project.

4. Design by feature. A 'design package' and a 'work package' is developed for each feature. Developers will put together sequence diagrams for each feature, and a 'design inspection' is held.

5. Build by feature. Assuming a successful design inspection, a feature (or 'client-valued function) is produced. The feature progresses through to unit testing and code inspection, and if considered complete, is merged with the main build.

FDD relies on a core set of engineering best practices, like code inspections and regular builds, all with the goal of delivering features and software that are valued by the client. Clients are to FDD what customers are to XP. It's a relatively simple and compelling methodology, but like all others it has its drawbacks. Following FDD, for example, requires the use of specialist tools like CASE Spec, a requirements management tool.

But it's biggest problem is that it draws its requirements from clients and businesses, not users. Sequencing features based on how much value they bring to the client - not the end user - is problematic. Sure, delivering business value is important and there is room in FDD to ask end users what they want, but the overall the methodology doesn't have an elegant way of balancing business needs against those of real users. Software is, at the end of the day, for people. Something's got to give.

Big design up front

Winston Royce, reluctant architect of the waterfall model, ironically favoured a software development methodology that was big on prototyping and iteration.

That methodology draws close parallels with what is today known as Big Design Up Front, or BDUF (sometimes also known as Big Modelling Up Front, or BMUF).

Less of a methodology on its own, BDUF is better described as a family of development methodologies that places high value on design and prototyping. The basic idea is to invest a substantial amount of energy (and resources) in designing and prototyping an application before actually building and testing it. Somewhat in contrast with waterfall, BDUF doesn't require every part of the architecture to be painstakingly predefined prior to build. Instead, the focus is on designing and thinking deeply about a product before building it to reduce the number of nasty surprises in development.

On his blog *Joel on Software*, Joel Spolsky describes using BDUF when writing the spec for Copilot.com, then known as Project Aardvark. After making some erroneous assumptions about port 443 and proxy servers, Spolsky and his team found themselves doing a lot of unplanned work prior to launching the final implementation of Copilot 1.0. The story reads like a project manager's nightmare, but in reality the extra work only added about ten per cent to the overall development effort.

"The reason you write a spec," says Spolsky "is not to solve every possible problem in advance."

> *"The reason you write a spec is to solve as many problems as you possibly can in advance so that you minimise the number of surprises that come up during development…Many times, thinking things out in advance saved us serious development headaches later on."*

For Spolsky, BDUF is the secret to saving time and making better products in the process. "I can't tell you how strongly I believe in Big Design Up Front," he writes. "I have consistently saved time and made better products by using BDUF and I'm proud to use it…"

Much like waterfall, the underlying premise of BDUF is that it's easier to fix a bug in the requirements phase than in the development phase. Adding extra, unplanned work during development is preferable to spending time debugging after a product has been shipped or implemented. And that makes sense.

But critics of BDUF argue, quite reasonably, that the Spolsky's method of choice shares the same drawbacks as its distant cousin, waterfall. Detractors of BDUF claim that extensive prototyping and designing makes it nearly impossible for large development projects to keep pace with changing business requirements or customer needs. Some go a step further and say that following BDUF reduces a team's willingness and ability to adapt to evolving requirements.

Critics have also argued that Spolsky's vision of the Big Design Up Front method isn't actually Big Design Up Front, and that it's more akin to an iterative approach. The introduction to the aforementioned Copilot.com spec even says:

"This specification is simply a starting point for the design of Aardvark 1.0, not a final blueprint. As we start to build the product, we'll discover a lot of things that won't work exactly as planned. We'll invent new features, we'll change things, we'll refine the wording, etc. We'll try to keep the spec up to date as things change. By no means should you consider this spec to be some kind of holy, cast-in-stone law."

Casting methodological purism aside, this brings to mind another point that BDUF critics raise: the method inevitably leads to a documentation burden. Energy spent designing is also energy spent documenting, recording and filing. This is especially true for projects plagued by a lack of comprehension or understanding of the actual requirements - which cynics would argue is every project.

There's also the issue of wastage. Some argue that the cost of planning and designing becomes an excessive overhead, especially if that cost begins to outweigh the cost of fixing a defect post-implementation. There's a risk that out of any number of weeks spent planning and prototyping, only one or two ideas will make it into development and even then, bugs may be still uncovered later on and additional resources will have to be deployed to fix it. In software, there's a limit to how prepared and proactive you can be.

So while Big Design Up Front has some influential supporters among its ranks, its use in the 'real world' is probably limited. That doesn't mean that contemporary software developers and project managers have thrown design out the window, however. There are still people out there who see the value in it.

Enter Scrum

We can look to Scrum for examples of such people. Scrum isn't a methodology; it's a framework for managing development projects and delivering quality products. The originators of the framework, Ken Schwaber and Jeff Sutherland, define Scrum as lightweight, simple to understand but difficult to master. In the Scrum Guide, the framework's proverbial bible, they explain:

> *"Scrum is not a process or a technique for building products; rather, it is a framework within which you can employ various processes and techniques. Scrum makes clear the relative efficacy of your product management and development practices so that you can improve."*

Fundamentally, scrum employs an iterative and incremental approach intended to 'optimise predictability' and 'control risk.' At the heart of this approach are three pillars: transparency, inspection and adaptation. There are also Scrum values, Scrum Teams and roles, Scrum Events and Scrum

Artefacts. You can probably also find Scrum t-shirts, mugs and stickers too.

The main principle underlying Scrum theory is empiricism, the assertion that knowledge comes from experience, and that decisions should be based on what is known. This is why Scrum places such high value on things like values and language; everyone in the project has to share a common understanding of what needs to be done, what is being done, and what 'done' even looks like.

When implemented properly, Scrum - unlike its BDUF or waterfall counterparts - supposedly helps projects cope with requirements volatility. The framework ensures that teams can adapt to changing requirements and still work productively, always delivering (incrementally) a useful version of a working product.

So where do design, planning and prototyping fit into this framework, if the focus is always on incremental delivery and adaptation? Where is the room for planning in a way of working that seemingly strips all sources of waste and delay from process?

The answer is quite simple. Scrum projects typically don't have an upfront design or planning phase, like BDUF or waterfall do. That would be antithetical to the values and pillars of Scrum. Rather design, just as everything else in Scrum, is iterative. A piecemeal development process isn't devoid of any design or planning work; in fact, the most successful 'Scrum-style' projects are those that approach design as an evolving piece of work, and as one component of the methodology they're using (remember Scrum is a framework, not a methodology). The point of Scrum is to do enough to get started, and to refine as you go. In this case, done is better than perfect.

There are more than a few problems with Scrum, and in our view it's a complete failure as far as frameworks go. With its rigid two-week development cycles, rituals, values, hierarchies and workflows, Scrum is a difficult thing to master. Unsurprisingly, it's rarely implemented as its founders intended.

Michael Church, programmer and writer of an eponymous blog described as a collection of 'rants, essays and diatribes,' penned an impressive takedown of Scrum in June, 2015. Church calls out Scrum for its problematic and difficult practices, and chief among his complaints is the fact that, in his view, scrum doesn't create an environment for technical excellence. In its pursuit of violent transparency and low autonomy, Scrum induces "needless anxiety" and never delivers on its promise of better, faster projects.

The biggest problem with Scrum, in our opinion, is that it is a guiding framework often followed as a recipe. Scrum is a collection of rituals, roles and artefacts - not an outlined process or methodology proper. And yet so many organisations have taken Scrum on board and 'followed' it something they read in Jamie Oliver's *30-Minute Meals*.

The result? Rituals become processes, and 'productivity' and velocity become sticks with which to beat developers. Mike Sutton, a British entrepreneur and founder of ScrumFest, captures it perfectly:

"Sprint after sprint, people do the meetings, the stand ups, the reviews etc. Scrum Masters – bless 'em – scour the communities for how to make their standups more interesting. Velocity is going up, teams are seven (plus or minus two) people strong – things in the product backlog read like 'As a …, I want…." The process seems to be working perfectly.

Yet software is still sitting on the shelf. Customers are not getting anything to feedback on. Developers still don't talk to customers."

That cuts to the essence of why Scrum fails. It's a framework, not a recipe, and it's not one that puts developers in front of users and customers. It's the same old snake oil wrapped up in funky, exotic terms and the latest buzzwords.

Emergent design

The point of Scrum, as we've said, is to approach tasks - including design ones - as evolving. In Scrum projects, teams do enough design and planning to get started on a product, and they refine as they go without investing huge amounts of time in planning up front.

This notion of design as an evolving process guided by development is central to the concept of 'emergent design.' Put simply, emergent design is the idea that the design of a product will emerge through its functionality. It's arguably the hallmark of lightweight development methodologies, and it's a simple idea in principle. Instead of investing resources in comprehensive design à la BDUF of waterfall, emergent design allows developers to begin building and delivering features from which a natural design will reveal itself. It reduces the risk of over-engineering a design or investing time in a less-than-ideal architecture. It also means less time spent preparing detailed design specifications.

But, as David Nicolette of *Leading Agile* has pointed out, letting a design 'emerge' through features can feel like pushing the north poles of two magnets together. They get close, but ultimately slide apart. The inherent risk of emergent design is that no usable, optimal design will actually emerge on its own. That's why test-driven development techniques are critical for the success of emergent design. But you know that already.

The death of Agile

In this chapter we have explored many of the noteworthy 'lightweight' methodologies, some of which pre-date Agile.

Why have we done this? Because in order to understand Agile and its demise, we need to understand where (and from whom) it came from. Alistair Cockburn puts it simply:

"The Agile Manifesto was the product of seventeen people from different schools and backgrounds. No one person is responsible for the words we came up with – it is clear that it was the product of all seventeen people. The addition or removal of any one person would have changed the outcome, something we recognised and discussed at the end of that meeting.

Whether you think 'Agile' saved the world or poisoned it, be sure always to recognise that it grew from a rich compost (joke intentional) of backgrounds. The next time you read a would-be history of the Agile movement, look for all those names. If you don't see them, it is not a history, it is one person's personal recounting of their own journey, years after the event (as indeed, this one is)."

Cockburn's statement gets to the heart of why Agile has died: few people understand or respect it for what it is, choosing instead to follow second-hand *interpretations* of the Agile Manifesto or, worse still, some management consultant's cheap imitation of it.

Agile failed not because it was inherently wrong or misguided. We said at the beginning of this chapter that the Agile Manifesto was an irrefutable thing of beauty, and its core values are spot-on. The problem with Agile is that was released into the wild and then co-opted by people unwilling and unable to really think about it or understand what it meant. Kent Beck calls this the 'staring dog problem.'

"If you try to point something out to a dog, it will look at your finger," he explains. "If you explain an idea in terms of concrete practices - like test driven development, pair programming, continuous integration - people will fixate on the practices and stop thinking."

Scrum and other lightweight spawns of Agile are failures precisely for this reason. They shroud important ideas like user centricity and fast iteration in practices, rituals, silly names and guiding principles. The Agile Manifesto itself, despite its brevity, left too much room for interpretation. And now it feels like we're back where we started in the late twentieth century with powerful technology, and no idea what to do with it.

Enabling the 3wks methodology

If you recall the second chapter of this book, you'll know that we created the 3wks methodology for several reasons:

1. We want to eliminate (or at least reduce) wastage in software development;

2. We want to create software that people actually use; and

3. We want to deliver projects on time and on budget.

An analysis of fifty thousand software projects conducted by The Standish Group found that in 2015, an average of just twenty-nine per cent of projects were successful (meaning they were delivered on time, on budget and to a satisfactory standard). Fifty-two per cent of projects, on the other hand, were 'challenged', and nineteen per cent were failed entirely.

That means that sixty-six per cent of all software projects were partial or complete failures.

It's no secret that software development projects, on the whole, are epic failures. Academics estimate the average rate of project failure on a global scale to be between thirty and seventy per cent. In a paper presented to the 7th International Conference on Knowledge Management in Organisations, Stanley and Uden proved that software projects typically overrun their budgets by two hundred per cent, and exceed their schedules by fifty.

But it's the *cost* of the failures that's the real issue here. The financial impact of project failure is no trivial thing. The data speaks for itself:

- In 2004, the total cost of project failure across the European Union was estimated at €142 billion;

- The cost of re-worked and abandoned systems costs the US economy an estimated $75 billion per year;

- In Australia, $5.4 billion is wasted each year on IT projects that don't deliver value or are abandoned completely;

- One project alone - the infamously abandoned National Health Service patient record system in the United Kingdom - cost taxpayers £10 billion.

To put those numbers into perspective, the United Nations estimates that a yearly investment of $267 billion would end world hunger by 2030. A meagre $175 billion per year would eliminate extreme poverty globally.

It's been a long time since the Agile Manifesto was written, and even longer since Winston Royce published *Managing the Development of Large Software Systems*. But nothing has changed and no single methodology has really improved software development. Software development is still a hugely expensive, wasteful endeavour that rarely meets expectations. And that's unacceptable.

The 3wks methodology won't solve world hunger or eradicate extreme poverty, but it does save money and reduce a waste in projects. We've used the methodology on hundreds of projects and each time, we've seen great results; 3wks projects, on the whole, are between twice or four times more capital efficient than others.

So how do we do it? The methodology on its own isn't what makes 3wks projects so successful. There's one essential tool that enables us to deploy releases within days of a project starting, and to deliver finished projects under budget. That tool is the cloud. Or, more specifically, the serverless cloud.

On the importance of pre-shaved yaks

There are three basic types of cloud services:

- Software as a Service (SaaS)

- Platform as a Service (PaaS)

- Infrastructure as a Service (IaaS)

The first type, SaaS, is familiar to just about anyone who has ever used a digital product. Third-party providers host applications and make them available to users over the internet, meaning organisations don't have to develop, install or run applications on their own machines or in their own data centres. In theory, this reduces the amount organisations have to spend on software licensing, support, hardware acquisition and all the rest.

The third type, IaaS, is the opposite of SaaS. This is a form of cloud computing that provides virtualised resources on the internet; in other words, its a computing infrastructure that is provisioned and managed by the user via some kind of online dashboard. The US National Institute of Standards and Technology (NIST) officially defines IaaS as:

"The capability provided to the consumer...to provision processing, storage, networks and other fundamental computing resources where the consumer is able to deploy and run arbitrary software, which can include operating systems and applications.

The consumer does not manage or control the underlying cloud infrastructure but has control over operating systems, storage and deployed applications; and possibly limited control of select networking components (e.g., host firewalls)."

With IaaS, you're getting virtualised hardware and raw components - CPU cores, servers and storage - and doing everything else yourself. The cloud service provider manages the hardware and virtualisation, but you're responsible for managing applications, database systems, middleware and operating systems. It's like using a self-service data centre.

IaaS is arguably the most popular type of cloud services among organisations and IT professionals. Indeed, according to RightScale's 2017 State of the Cloud Report, ninety-five per cent of organisations are running applications (or experimenting) with IaaS. At face-value it's easy to see why IaaS is so en vogue: it sidesteps the upfront expense of setting up and managing an old-school data centre, and its service level agreement (SLA) reduces the cost of business continuity and disaster recovery. Furthermore, IaaS use is metered like electricity and other utilities, so users only pay for the capacity they need at a given time. This kind of pay-as-you-go model is what makes IaaS attractive to so many.

But what advocates of this type of cloud service have failed to account for are the human and financial costs of designing, provisioning and maintaining infrastructure. They celebrate the flexibility and 'customisability' of IaaS offerings but forget that with great power comes great responsibility.

With IaaS, DevOps teams are needed to deploy each service, configure interfaces and application runtime, manage instances, take responsibility for scaling and manually patch operating systems when there are critical updates. And that's just a few items off the task list. Running a project using an IaaS solution, therefore, requires people who understand how to manage it. It also requires more time in the schedule to account for the days or weeks needed to provision and test the IaaS setup.

This is why we don't use IaaS. Using an IaaS solution would make it impossible for us to release working software to users within days of a project's initial kick-off, and it would increase the cost of projects substantially. We wouldn't have to provision and set up hardware, sure, but we'd still have to cover the cost of DevOps and account for the time they'd need to spend yak shaving before the developers could even begin coding. Put frankly, if we were to use IaaS solutions, we'd be failing in our mission to reduce wastage and slowness in software development. The point of our methodology would be lost.

So we use Platform as a Service (PaaS) solutions instead. In the PaaS model, the provisioning and operation of an application's underlying infrastructure is fully automated. As a developer, you don't have to manage or control underlying infrastructure (including network, servers, operating systems or storage) but you retain control over any deployed applications. The PaaS provider provisions and manages low-level infrastructure resources, but also provides a fully-functioning application development and deployment platform complete with middleware, tools and managed services. This is something you don't get with an IaaS provider.

In PaaS environments, developers are removed from the gritty realities of infrastructure and left to focus on the really important things, like developing and deploying software. Developers don't need to concern themselves with how or where infrastructure resources are provisioned; they can rely on the PaaS providers to take care of that. Plus, they can leverage pre-configured application environments to quickly and develop application with a fairly complex deployment topology - all without the need for DevOps. That's a win for productivity and expenditure.

In a nutshell, PaaS reduces the time and resources needed to develop software. With resource allocation, capacity planning and environment creation largely left to the service provider, PaaS enables organisations and developers to focus on core activities. The result? Faster time to market and projects that come in under budget.

Counting the benefits of PaaS

Back in the 'old' days it would take weeks to provision, test and deploy infrastructure to developers. When you add that to the time already taken earlier in the project to gather requirements and agree on deliverables, about three months (and around $100, 000) is spent with no software or value to show for it. It's sheer wastage, pure and simple.

Infrastructure as a Service has done a lot to reduce the effort and cost involved in setting up architecture and running projects, but it's not enough. It still requires huge expenditure in the form of time, money and manpower. And given that the likelihood and cost of project failure is statistically astronomical, these are additional costs we'd prefer to avoid - especially if they're not needed in the first place.

This is why we advocate the use of Platform as a Service. With PaaS we can save time and money, and we can focus solely on developing great software and delivering business benefits. It takes mere minutes to provision an infrastructure with a PaaS provider, and just about anyone can do it - there's no need for architects, system administrators or network engineers.

PaaS is our secret to eliminating wastage in software development. Without it, we wouldn't be able to deploy rapidly or run capital-efficient projects. We've run nearly two hundred projects on a mix of IaaS and PaaS, and PaaS comes out on top every time. Don't believe it? We've crunched the numbers on our own projects to prove it.

Evaluating PaaS versus IaaS

Using a sample of one hundred and eighty enterprise projects completed since 2012, we've demonstrated (to ourselves and our clients, at the very least) that PaaS is the way forward.

The projects analysed represent a cross-section of our clients and generally involved the development of some sort of digital business solution, often with thousands of end users and integrations into core platforms like Salesforce and SAP. Roughly two thirds of the projects involved automating various business processes to reduce costs, and others were entirely new digital products. In sixty per cent of the projects we built enterprise web solutions with a Java backend; the remaining forty per cent were iOS and Android apps, also with a Java backend. The median project size was around $300,000, with an upper bound of around $4 million.

Here's what our analysis found:

- Projects run on PaaS cost up to fifty per cent less than those run in IaaS;

- Operating costs dropped by eighty per cent in PaaS projects when compared with IaaS projects;

- When asked to quote on projects using IaaS, the total cost of a project was upwards of three times higher than it would normally be with PaaS; and

- Nearly one hundred per cent of our IaaS projects suffered an overrun because we had to wait for clients to provision and deploy infrastructure before we could begin coding.

What's also clear from our experience that automation plays a big role not just in cutting project costs, but also in reducing post-project operating costs. Take the example of a system we built for a government client: the four thousand-user system required three sets of infrastructure or 'environments' for development, testing and producing. Our PaaS provider was charging $600 per month in hosting costs, which included administration staff. At our client's request (and against our advice), we moved the system over to IaaS and the monthly cost escalated to $4,500. That's excluding the additional $1,500 (which is a conservative estimate) our client would have spent on staff required to maintain the infrastructure. If they'd followed our advice and stuck with PaaS, they would have benefit from a ninety per cent saving.

IaaS solutions cost more because there is a base charge for using their compute power, and in enterprise projects the per-machine mandatory spend adds up fast. Most PaaS services, in contrast, are able to suspend processes when they're not in use (say, during the night when the majority of the user base is asleep) which results in an overall lower operational cost.

The way forward

According to market intelligence firm Global Industry Analysts Inc. the PaaS market is projected to reach $7.5 billion in value by 2020.

The key drivers of this growth include the global trend towards developing custom software (instead of buying packaged or 'off the shelf' software), a growing focus on cloud integration, and a recognised need to reduce wastage and costs. RightScale research has found that between thirty and forty-five per cent of cloud spend is wasted, and more than fifty per cent of enterprise cloud users cite 'optimising cloud costs' as a key initiative.

But despite its bright future and many obvious benefits , PaaS is currently shunned by many in the software community. Enterprise adoption of DevOps rose to eighty-four per cent in 2016, and IaaS remains the solution of choice.

The reason for this is quite simple: PaaS has made automation more affordable than the IT professionals previously required to provision and manage infrastructure. But in most organisations, these are the people who have authority over decisions about infrastructure and architecture. In our experience, at least one third of enterprises are at the mercy of solutions designers, administrators and people in various architecture roles. Every single one of them has a vested interest in making sure PaaS never makes it through the door.

Some organisations, however, have seen the light. Speaking to Stratoscale, Roger Strukhoff (former Director of Research at software development company, Altoros Systems) said that his company had found "that the key difference between IaaS and PaaS deployment is that a highly competent DevOps team needs to be in place when deploying on infrastructure, where as a platform-based approach manages most operational details."

"With the PaaS approach, the platform itself controls application lifecycles and scaling, automatically deploys the application runtime, uses containers to manage instances as isolated elements, and more.

We don't necessarily think an IaaS-focussed approach is all bad. We understand that many enterprises are successfully working directly with infrastructure through their DevOps teams. But it can get ugly if you're not rigorous with creating a sophisticated DevOps team."

Altoros strongly believes in the power of PaaS in deploying modern enterprise IT solutions, and Strukhoff's comments echo those of other enlightened professionals. By lowering the cost of automation, PaaS is presenting itself as an attractive alternative to IaaS, SaaS and FaaS (Framework as a Service).

The road to PaaS adoption

Kent Beck, the brains behind extreme programming, says that 'responsible development' is the style of development he now aspires to in the twenty-first century:

"It can be summarised by answering the question: how would I develop if it were my money? I'm amazed by how many theoretical arguments evaporate when faced with this question."

Software projects are often treated like mystical, complex activities that only those endowed with certain skills and knowledge can control. They're subject to the wants and desires of all-powerful IT departments, who are supposedly the only ones capable of running software projects. We see this kind of attitude everywhere, especially in organisations practising lean and Agile methodologies. For these people, software development is sacred.

But it's not. Software development is like any other business project and it needs to be held accountable as such. This is why, in our experience, it's the business people - like Chief Financial Officers - who are the voice of reason in software projects.

Software development projects are, and always have been, about money. The very point of most projects is to make money. But many organisations and IT professionals have lost sight of this, and that's why we've seen so many projects overrun budgets and schedules. If you questioned the logic behind an organisation's decision to use IaaS, a solutions architect would likely quote 'total cost of ownership', without knowing what that total cost actually is. It is the ultimate bluff, and one that is no longer acceptable in a world where so much money is wasted on software that never sees the light of day.

Now, more than ever, we're seeing CFOs and other decision-makers take the lead in arbitrating technology decisions. In our opinion, this is the right approach to running software projects. To be successful, IT needs to relearn the vocabulary of business and money, and remove IT jargon from the process.

Making the 3wks methodology possible

Everyone from Jeff Gothelf and Marc Andreessen to Satya Nadella and Marco Annunziata has said that every company needs to become a software company. And Adam Gross, CEO of Heroku, agrees.

Speaking at San Francisco's DeveloperWeek conference in 2017, Gross told attendees that in today's world, even companies not known for producing software need to be as good at operating customer-facing applications as Amazon, Facebook or Google. But to do that, software development needs to be easier:

"How are they going to absorb all that complexity and sophistication?" he asked. "It's not going to be by starting at the bottom of the stack."

PaaS, Gross argues, is a growth driver for organisations. It's what makes it possible to build and release customer-ready applications without protracted timelines and enormous budgets.

It's also what makes it possible for us at 3wks to start a project on Monday and have a first release ready by Wednesday. It's also the reason why we're able to deliver projects significantly under budget. Our clients and even our developers are surprised by our ability to work so quickly (and so cheaply) but it wouldn't be possible without PaaS.

With PaaS, we can allocate almost one hundred per cent of a project's budget to producing deliverable, high-quality code. We don't have to sacrifice time, money or resources on mind-numbing infrastructure tasks that can easily be automated. We can focus on the important things, and eliminate wastage in the process.

So here's the bottom line: to use the 3wks methodology and move beyond Agile, you need to go serverless and embrace PaaS. You also need to get IT talking in financial terms, and you need to get business decisions makers to arbitrate technological decisions. Complex projects, overrun schedules and blown budgets are nothing to be proud of, especially when we could feed the world's starving masses with the amount we waste on failed projects.

Still learning

By the end of 2012 we had discovered a way of working that enabled us to actually deliver products and solve customer problems. We were able to deliver usable products within days or weeks of receiving a brief, and we were putting users at the centre of the process.

Best of all, we'd found a way of working that kept us sane and enabled us to transcend the usual minutiae of normal projects: business cases, project plans, roadmaps, timelines, etcetera.

There was just one problem.

Finding people (clients, no less) who understood what we were doing was proving to be a challenge. From our perspective, with our value proposition and unique working methods, 3wks was an easy sell. What organisation *wouldn't* want to partner with a company that could solve real problems and create usable products in such a short timeframe, and usually at a fraction of the expected cost? Many organisations, apparently.

Classical economists often cite rational choice theory when trying to explain how and why people make certain decisions. Consumers, theory says, are rational beings. They make purchasing decisions by weighing their options using all available information, and they choose a product or a service that is utility-maximising; in other words, they pick the one that gets them the most bang for their buck.

Rational choice theory provides a neat, simple lens through which to analyse consumer decision-making, but it ultimately fails to explain how real people make decisions. Daniel McFadden, a Nobel Prize-winning economist, has written extensively about this. Speaking to *The Atlantic* in 2013, he explains:

"…Neither the physiology of pleasure nor the methods we use to make choices are as simple or as single-minded as the classical economists thought. A lot of behaviour is consistent with pursuit of self-interest, but in novel or ambiguous decision-making environments there is a good chance that our habits will fail us and inconsistencies in the way we process information will undo us."

"Trade is a contest, with a chance of coming out on the short end. Animals in 'fight or flee' situations often find it safer to flee. Similarly, people in situations where trade is possible, or even promising, may find it safer to turn away. It takes trust to trade."

Choice is good, yes. But as economists like McFadden have found, it's physically exhausting. Humans don't like having to make decisions, so we turn to habits and heuristics to shortcut the whole process and stick to what we know. Something that is unusual, like a company promising to deliver an app in three weeks, requires processing power that we simply sometimes don't have.

Notable psychologist Daniel Kahneman explores this in his best-selling book *Thinking, Fast and Slow*. He calls it the 'law of least effort':

> *"A general 'law of least effort' applies to cognitive as well as physical exertion. The law asserts that if there are several ways of achieving the same goal, people will eventually gravitate to the least demanding course of action. In the economy of action, effort is a cost, and the acquisition of skill is driven by the balance of benefits and costs. Laziness is built deep into our nature."*

This was a revelation for us. The problem wasn't that we were working with inherently lazy people or organisations who 'just didn't get us' - in fact, the opposite was true. Our problem was that in the process of finding clients and collaborators, we were skipping a crucial requirement: common ground.

Shared values and ideas are the foundation for a successful partnership. Our entire method of working is grounded in accountability; we need to be able to make decisions, and our clients need to be empowered to do the same. We needed to find partners that weren't just willing to work with us, but ones who really wanted to change the way their organisations developed and delivered products. We realised that a mutual desire to change and innovate was essential for project success, and for securing repeat business.

Finding clients that ticked all those boxes felt like searching for phytoplankton in the ocean without a microscope. We knew they existed, but we couldn't see them. That's why, when Monash University's newly-minted

CIO reached out to us in 2015, we breathed a sigh of gratitude and relief.

Monash University was established 1958 with a vision of becoming a research-focused institution focusing on science and technology, but on its website the University boasts of how it "quickly moved beyond the bounds of expectation."

> *"Free from tradition and convention, we were within just a few years of our first intake of a mere 347 students, offering courses in arts, economics, education, engineering, law, medicine, politics and science."*

That's quite a lineup for a small, relatively nascent institution like Monash. Perhaps its culture of "creativity, innovation and irreverence" is what gave it the ability to eschew traditional teaching methods and expand its course catalog within a number of decades. Perhaps that culture is also what enabled the University to become the epicentre of student radicalism in Australia during the 1960s and 1970s, and later - in the 1990s - expand rather aggressively (through a series of mergers) to eventually become one of the nation's largest public research institutions.

One thing we know for certain is that culture of creativity and innovation persists today, and it's the one of the key reasons why Trevor Woods was so drawn to Monash when the University offered him the role of Chief Information Officer (CIO) in 2015.

"The culture is one that resonates with me" he says. "We want to be excellent and enterprising, international and inclusive, and reach out to the community to make a better world."

"These characteristics exemplify who I am and the kind of university community I want to serve. I want to help build teams with the right people and culture to accomplish this."

Woods, a native of Canada, is best described as the kind of guy you'd want to work for or have a drink with. He's intelligent, approachable, pragmatic - a natural fit for a place like Monash. Indeed, before relocating to Melbourne he served as Executive Director, Information Services and Technology, at the University of Alberta.

There he was tasked with the simple brief: transform the University's IT. When he joined in 2010 the University's IT budget was impossibly stretched across fifty independent business units, each with its own team of staff totalling over five hundred people. There was little alignment between IT objectives and the University's broader goals and, as is the case for many organisations, the notion of using IT to deliver better outcomes for customers, students or staff was almost a foreign one.

Woods wasted no time getting to work. In just five years he managed to unite the University's IT resources and made IT the foundation for transformation across the institution's other business units. His team put more tech in classrooms, deployed the G Suite for Education (formerly known as Google Apps of Education), and won Pink Elephant's 2012 ITIL Project Of The Year award. The sheer scale of the University's transformation is incredible.

And with a track record like that, it's easy to see why Woods was an ideal candidate for the challenging CIO role in the much larger, albeit younger, Monash University.

We first met Woods in August 2015 when he was still relatively new to Monash, a place he described as big, bureaucratic and in many ways traditional. He was coming to grips with Melbourne (having only just moved there in June) and was searching for someone, anyone, who could help him challenge the status quo.

"I was looking for people or companies that could help us figure out how to work differently," he says, reflecting on the origins of our relationship.

"I wanted to get away from multi-year projects that relied on that traditional waterfall approach where you try to figure everything out and then execute, regardless of what you learn along the way."

"I needed to be able to start delivering solutions much faster, within days or weeks, without overcomplicating it. And when I put the word out and started asking around, someone mentioned 3wks. The rest is history. "

Our initial meeting with Woods quickly revealed that we were on the same page when it came to how we work, and what we were trying to achieve. So we started looking for a low-risk project within the University that we could cut our teeth on. Woods talked to the Dean at the beginning of the week and by Wednesday we were in a room with a programme director.

They explained their problem to us carefully. It seemed that around eight independent processes in the University's graduate research departments were using a convoluted form to manage simple requests from higher degree research students. This form had complicated, nearly nonsensical logic and required a string of approvals from various managers and departments. Completed forms would often end up on an journey that rivalled that of Odysseus himself, usually getting lost in the process. In some cases they made their way back to students weeks late, and with the wrong signatures.

What we had here was relatively simple process made needlessly complicated by paperwork. So we fixed it.

We built a website with some simple logic. A student would enter their phone number and outline the nature of their request. That request would then be forwarded to the relevant approver, and both student and approver would get a text message. The fastest approval, according to Woods, was in single digit minutes.

So we had sat down on Wednesday to receive our brief and by Friday, we had a fully functioning alpha build of the website that leveraged the Google platform. Within another week we were ready to release.

"We'd created a perfectly working system that replaced the paper process in almost no time at all," says Woods.

"Something that would takes weeks to approve and often get lost is now being approved within minutes or hours. It's a much better experience for the students, and for University staff.'

"That early project helped us build credibility internally," he explains. "We realised that we had something good going, and we needed to start communicating that across the business."

After the success of our initial project for Monash, Woods began identifying more projects for us to work on. Some were larger projects with iterations being delivered every week or two, as part of bigger initiatives across the University. Others were smaller, almost ad-hoc projects.

"I've stopped keeping track of how many projects you guys work on," Woods laughs. "It's probably dozens by now."

"But I remember one Tuesday afternoon I had an idea to try a 'pop-up' innovation, rapid development thing," he says animatedly.

"The idea was to get some smart developers, let them set up shop somewhere on campus and get them talking to students about what their pain points are, and what apps and services they'd like to see."

"My thinking was that based on those conversations, the devs could pick a problem and start building an application to solve that."

"Nothing like that had ever been done at the University but after I'd thought of it, the whole thing just took off. You guys had a team and a video crew down here by Tuesday night and you were talking to students, trying to really understand what they needed. It all happened so fast."

It really did. We were given a week to solve a single problem for Monash students and we had to work fast. A 3wks team landed on campus, camera crew in tow, and we started canvassing students to discover a problem they could (hopefully) solve.

As we anticipated, there was a lot of variety in the responses we got. Some students complained about Moodle, a learning management system being used by various departments in the University. Others wanted a portal for information about events and activities happening on campus. A few students said they needed help finding study spaces on campus.

But out of the spectrum of responses we received there emerged what seemed to be a fairly common problem: students were having trouble finding and accessing computer labs on campus. There was no way to know whether a particular computer lab had any available seats, or which labs had Macs or PCs. And with demand for seats so high, finding a lab facility was a frustrating experience.

So we started building a simple web app that would make it easy for the students to locate, compare and book seats in computer labs across campus. They could search by location and even narrow their search to find labs that had printers, Macs, chargers, or even computers equipped with specialist software. It turned the experience of finding a seat in a computer lab - which was a bit like trial and error, or sheer guesswork - into a simple, intuitive process akin to making an online hotel reservation. For the students, many of them young digital natives, we had solved one of their most pervasive problems with a familiar, functional product.

But we realised that for the project to be successful, we couldn't just engage students at the beginning of the process and then forget about them. We had to involve students at every step of the journey, from design and the build through to testing and release.

Fortunately, the pace we working at made this possible. We worked feature by feature, hour by hour, creating space for a continuous feedback loop. We would work on one feature, test it on a real student, and iterate accordingly.

We couldn't have overestimated the value of incorporating student feedback at every step of the process. They had so many insights and ideas that we, being personally removed from the problem and only having just become exposed to it, likely wouldn't have thought of ourselves.

One student, for example, pointed out that the booking system should allow for intervals between bookings so that students have time to vacate their seats or, on the other hand, get to the lab and set up before their allotted time begins. Another student pointed out that access to some buildings and computer labs is restricted to students in particular departments or degree programmes. How would we have known that if we hadn't asked for her input?

Involving students in the design, build and testing of the app meant that by the end of the week, we had built a functional product that students actually needed, and one they wanted to use. When trying the final release of the app for the first time, one student described it as 'absolutely perfect.'

"I'm so excited about this," she said. "This is exactly what we need."

"It doesn't seem like a big deal but it was," says Woods. "Our whole journey with 3wks has started a counterculture; we're no longer doing things the way they used to. There are no business cases or two-year plans. We just show up, look at the problem and then produce the results."

"And I really like that we're sort of flying under the radar on this. Our approach is substance over sizzle. We're just spending our time getting the real work done rather than talking about what it is that we hope to achieve. We focus on getting the hard yards done and actually making things better for the students and the staff."

Upon reflection, Woods is quick to point out that the value in our way of working goes beyond the ability to 'do stuff quickly.' The real value, he says, is in how we bring a different approach and way of thinking to problem solving in general.

"You guys helped us understand what is technically possible, but I think the real powerful learning was that we didn't need fifteen or eighteen months to build something."

"It sounds crazy but in an organisation like this with lots of late-career professionals who are used to a culture of risk mitigation, that's a big shift."

Has it been a painful shift? Woods says no. In fact, the shift in mindset and approach has allowed Monash to quickly identify more core process problems, work with the people directly affected by those problems, and come up with functional, effective solutions to those problems.

Monash University's experience cuts to the essence of our approach and highlights its core benefit. It doesn't just make it easy to create products on a shorter timeframe. Rather, it changes the way organisations think about problem-solving and development overall. It makes them reassess their own internal capabilities, and what they need to do to fundamentally transform how they operate.

"Our end goal is an overall transformation in how we deliver student services," says Woods.

> *"The beyond Agile approach, right from the beginning, gave us a set of ideas that are instrumental in the grander scheme of achieving organisational change."*

This journey, Woods says, isn't really about methodologies. "It's about embedding your particular approach and way of thinking into our organisational culture to effect widespread change in our operations."

Eventually, Woods will look to expand the University's internal capabilities in order to deliver on projects and create products without the need for partners or external developers.

"Historically we just didn't have the resources or the buy-in to do projects like the ones we've been doing with 3wks," he says. "And that's why we're looking to build capability internally."

Woods is blunt: "I don't want to become dependent on external providers to deliver better outcomes for students, but it's necessary for now."

"There are people who think it costs more to engage external developers but from my perspective, that cost should always be thought of in terms of return on investment.

"Being able to get a better solution faster, for often less money in total, means you've spent less money over a longer period of time and you can see your return almost immediately. For us that's brilliant because traditionally it's taken years to see a return on an IT investment!"

For us, hearing Woods recount his experience with 3wks and his plans for the future engenders a feeling that's almost like empty nest syndrome. The foundation of our business has historically been software development; clients pay us to make things for them, and we conceptualise work in terms of individual projects.

So what happens when clients start making things themselves?

We complain and wax lyrical about stodgy organisations that embark upon huge, uninspired projects, but one could argue that we profit off that. We talk about needing to find clients and partners who share our values and understand how we work, but we make money off teaching them our ways too.

It would be easy to discourage people like Trevor Woods from expanding his organisation's internal capabilities and building products on his own. But the reality is that we don't just encourage our clients do that, we help them do it. Why?

There are many reasons. A cynical one would be that we can't (and don't want to) spend the rest of our lives building apps for clients unwilling to lift a finger or two of their own.

Another, perhaps more credulous reason is that we can't advance a methodology and approach to software development that values innovation and customer centricity without actually *encouraging* those values in the organisations we work with.

But the chief reason behind our willingness to help our clients transform their organisations, and ultimately reach a stage where they no longer need our help, is the fact that software is about people. The problems it solves are real people's problems. It's created by people, funded by people, and used by people.

Discouraging innovation and growth in the organisations we work with might create opportunities for us to do work for them, but it would result in the inevitable failure of our approach. Going beyond Agile requires a change in thinking across the board. It's not enough for us to be working this way; to be successful, we need others to do it too.

Abraham Maslow, the famed creator of the eponymous hierarchy of needs, once said that in any given moment we have two options: to step forward into growth, or to step back into safety. Change, as we know, is inevitable. But growth is optional.

We're of the opinion that the world and those who live in it will evolve, adapt and change whether we like it or not. That's why we, like Trevor Woods, don't see the 'beyond Agile' approach as just another methodology or a set of practices. It's a tool for coping with change, and ultimately shaping it. It's a way to change how people conceptualise and solve problems.

But that begs the question: if the core of the approach is changing how people approach and solve problems, how much of its success depends on actual people *themselves?*

A cat among the pigeons

A rthur Miller, one of the great American playwrights of the 20th century, once wrote that "the structure of a play is always the story of how the birds came home to roost."

"The hidden," he declared in his essay *The Shadows of the Gods* published August 1958 issue of Harper's Magazine, "will be unveiled; the inner laws of reality will announce themselves…"

Miller was largely talking about his impressions of 1929 and the Great Depression, but he was also speaking to his broader understanding of life itself. For Miller, our history, our choices and our futures are irrevocably linked. In *Death of a Salesman*, Willy's dreams and ambitions inevitably shape Biff's life. And in *All My Sons*, the interplay between choice and consequence takes centre stage throughout.

After a few years of developing, formalising and practising the 3wks methodology, we found ourselves constantly faced with choices, consequences and the space between them. Had we really found something that worked, or was there more to do? Should we declare victory and go home, or keep refining something we'd already spent years formulating?

The 3wks methodology, as we've said ad nauseam, isn't written in stone. It has its essential principles and working practices that we do our best to abide by, but following the methodology isn't an exercise in purism. It's simply an exercise in delivering real products to real people, in the best ways possible.

That opens a lot of doors to companies that want to sign up to the 3wks experience, but perhaps can't commit to all its values and requirements. In advancing the methodology and bringing it into various organisations, we eventually found ourselves *teaching* as well as *doing*. We were showing our clients how they could practise the 3wks methodology on their own, and time and time again we were hearing people like Trevor Woods say that their focus is on 'building internal capability.' Organisations were taking our methodology, adjusting its flavour and making it palpable for their palates.

We have learned by now that for the 3wks methodology to be successful it needs to be layered over the right mix of people, in a particular set of circumstances. There have been times where it worked and times where it hasn't, and that's okay. But at some point we began to ask ourselves some rather existential questions:

1. Is the 3wks methodology perennial or ephemeral? What's the shelf life of a methodology anyway?

2. Can it survive if it's being practised in part, but not in whole? Will it become diluted to the point where it is more an idea, less a working methodology? Is it destined for the same fate as (the supposedly dead) Agile? Should we intervene?

We hoped that in some sort of Miller-esque way, the answers to these grand questions would reveal themselves in time. But we also realised that in the present, we have the ability to shape the future of the methodology. There was a choice to be made: be uncompromising in our application of the methodology and rule its users with an iron fist, or relax and help organisations find a way to make it work for them.

News Corp helped us decide.

Breaking News

Tom Quinn had taken on the role of News Corp's Chief Technology Officer in 2004, six years before Andrew joined the business as an Agile delivery manager. Under Quinn, News Corp underwent what would become a decade-long transformation that included, among other things, an aggressive move to the cloud and an overhaul of legacy systems.

By 2015, nearly eighty per cent of the company's platforms had been moved to third-party, cloud-based infrastructure, and twelve legacy content management systems (CMS) had been replaced with a single CMS.

News Corp's strategy, Quinn told attendees of 2015 APIDays conference in Sydney, was to be 'atomised' and cloud-first. He said they had split (figuratively speaking) the business environment into functions that he likened to Lego blocks. The idea, he explained, was to use various cloud systems to run each of these blocks - and to swap them out if something better came along.

"Some services you will deploy and be disappointed with," he told the audience. "So you'll have to pull them and put something else in. It's a continually moving feast."

A moveable feast indeed. The new strategy had enabled News Corp to embrace innovative technologies and become a lot more nimble on the whole, but it wasn't without its problems. In a patchwork system of atomised business units and cloud services, there was a risk that something or someone would fall through the cracks.

"If you've atomised your business and you've got a number of different services providing an end-to-end process for the business, there are gaps in between those services," said Quinn.

And so the company began focusing on what Quinn described as the 'glue' or the stitching that would bind its various cloud-based systems and business units together. That glue, he explained, wasn't just made up of technology. It included people too.

When Quinn departed News Corp the following year in 2016, the company's former Head of Digital Product Development, Alisa Bowen, took over. And with new leadership came a new organisational structure.

The publisher merged its formerly separate technology and digital teams into a single unit reporting into Bowen, bringing internal and customer-facing IT services into one division of the business. She recounted the story for us over the phone one afternoon:

"In the previous era, tech and product teams were like separate organisations. And the outcome of that was a whole group of different product managers, each responsible for designing consumer requirements and business models - but separate from customers, and the engineers who were actually building the products.

The gulf between those two groups meant our turnaround times were slow, and we suffered from chronic miscommunication."

But was it all bad? No, says Bowen. The somewhat haphazard structure forced teams to communicate and keep each other in check. It had, in some respects, a built-in system of checks and balances.

"I suppose an upshot of that structure was that it created a layer of management. Teams were babysitting each other, doing their best to stay in touch with the rest of the business, ensuring requirements were well coordinated and that roadmaps were delivered.

But for the most part it was terribly inefficient, and it was unfulfilling for the people involved in delivering digital products and services. Nobody in tech or product felt empowered. We all felt like our efforts to put the customer at the centre of our products were being compromised because of internal bridges and the way we organised ourselves."

In restructuring its tech and product divisions, News Corp effectively redefined innovation on its own terms. Innovation was no longer something espoused and practised in the organisation by isolated pockets of tech geeks. Rather, innovation began to look more like the recombination of ideas, people and capabilities in ways that create value. And that definition, Bowen says, is one that everyone in the organisation could relate to and embrace.

Recounting the experience to news.com.au (ahead of her appearance at Pivot Summit in December, 2016) Bowen explained the core intent behind the restructure and the company's innovation agenda:

"We specifically avoided creating a dedicated team that could be misinterpreted as the only people in the company that had a licence to be innovative," she said.

"Everything we have done has been about inclusiveness and trying to provide the tools, the techniques and the freedom for that innovation to happen."

She had said a similar thing to us just a month prior, in a conversation that highlighted what Bowen considers to be two of her most valuable assets: talent and customers.

Talented people, in Bowen's opinion, are the most critical resource an organisation has, and she'd shill out for exceptional talent any day of the week. Historically speaking, News Corp's reputation for torpidity and lack of creativity has made it difficult for the company to attract the best talent. The move to more Agile working practices is, she says frankly, a weapon in the war for talent.

But customers matter just as much, if not more. Indeed, the drive to attract top talent is largely about attracting passionate people who sincerely want to make a difference for consumers.

Evidently, 'the customer' is not an abstraction and customer-centricity is not a gimmick for Bowen; it's a strategy that's of paramount importance. Ahead of her appearance at the Public Relations Institute of Australia (PRIA) conference in 2015, Bowen was asked by the Institute's then marketing and communications manager, Neil O'Sullivan, to consider a hypothetical situation:

"If there was a fight between a journalist, a marketer, a PR professional, an advertiser, a tech guru, a digital whizz and a creative, what tool would you bring to the fight? And who would win?" O'Sullivan asked.

Her answer? The customer.

"I'd bring the customer into the room," she said.

> *"The customer has no axe to grind - they just want their needs met with the least hassle and cost, and anyone in the fight who's not helping can leave the room."*

Bowen's straightforward, customer-focussed and 'take no prisoners' brand of leadership perhaps explains how she's managed to achieve so much in her career. After leaving Melbourne and her hometown of regional Mildura, she pursued an MBA and eventually joined multinational mass media company Thomson Reuters as a business analyst. She spent a over a decade there working her way up to the role of Senior Vice President and Head of Business Operations, accumulating list of accomplishments as she went. Among many other things, Bowen oversaw the redesign of Reuters. com, launched various mobile applications in seventeen countries and grew the company's global consumer audience by over fifty per cent in just two years.

She then departed for Dow Jones where she served as General Manager for the Wall Street Journal Digital Network, and eventually Chief Product Officer. When she was hired, the publisher's then-President, Todd Larsen, said that Bowen possessed the background and skills needed to "expand the digital potential" of the company's existing brands and to "continue to pioneer new products and platforms."

News Corp's senior leadership team undoubtedly thought the same when it tapped Bowen for the role of Quinn's replacement at the beginning of 2016. But, like Trevor Woods of Monash University, the newly-minted CTO couldn't embark on the next chapter of the company's digital transformation without some help. And that's where we came in.

"When we turned to 3wks, News Corp had already combined the tech and digital product teams into one unit," she explains.

"As a unit they were tasked with equipping the business with the technology it needs to deliver products. The tech team is responsible for internal platforms, and the product teams are responsible for external platforms - like our websites, mobile sites and apps.

"We had eliminated an overhead in the form of internal stakeholder management, and we really wanted to empower our teams. In projects we wanted them define the outcomes and own the delivery of those outcomes, end-to-end.

But we were asking for a big cultural change on top of an organisational, structural change. It was difficult at first and we had to find a way to get everyone on board."

Bowen turned to 3wks in search of what she described as 'a cat to put amongst the pigeons.' She needed a group of people, external to the business, to come in and disrupt how News Corp's tech and product teams were working and thinking about products.

At first, we were brought into create (or fill gaps) in the organisation's capabilities. We were asked to deliver a framework for the beta version of the company's content APIs and though it was a relatively modest project, it had a significant impact on the way the business went about problem solving.

"That first project paved the way for a different way of thinking across the teams," says Bowen. "It helped accelerate our thinking in the areas of APIs, and it showed our staff that there are different ways to solve and approach problems."

"But most of all," she continues "it opened the door for new capabilities to brought in, and it allowed us to overcome residual resistance to change internally."

"By exposing the team to a way of working that focuses relentlessly on customer value, I think we showed people that you can do away with many of the roadblocks that bog down large organisations like News. You can create products in a rapid timeframe, and you can do it in a way that has no time or space for exhaustive process or internal politics."

Following the success of our initial project, we were given another job: to make it easy for advertisers to buy print advertising space. It wasn't a difficult problem in a conceptual sense, but News Corp had already tried and failed to find a successful solution to it. In the end, we settled on a simple self-service platform that let advertisers buy and manage print space across News Corp's titles.

Then came another project. Mark Drasutis, who was then Head of Innovation (and is now the company's Chief Product Officer, Digital) asked us to help him develop a new and innovative product in the lifestyle space. The request, he said, came largely from advertisers who were seeking more opportunities for engagement beyond News Corp's existing product offering.

Going into this project, we had one key hypothesis: that providing users with a richer, more engaging and complete experience in the lifestyle space would increase the likelihood of them completing a transaction. So we worked with that hypothesis, and built a product - several products, actually - to resolve it. Subsequent projects with Drasutis and the innovation team built on this foundation, and we found ourselves collaborating with *The Australian and Daily Telegraph* and creating long form, rich media content and mobile web apps across the lifestyle categories.

Our success with Drasutis and these projects largely came down to the fact that the 3wks methodology was well suited for it. More often than not there was a clear problem, a workable hypothesis and an outcome we could reasonably contract to. These were also projects that we were involved in right from the beginning - something, you'll recall from Chapter Two, we identify as a critical indicator of a project's likely success.

"You were part of the creative design and commercial thinking process up front," says Drasutis. And because of that, we could "get started much earlier, move faster and create better products."

Recalling this experience with innovation team, Bowen describes the projects as a good case study in just how much can be achieved when the 3wks methodology is used to change thinking, not just build products.

Whatever works

"Things started to take off when we started leveraging the 3wks methodology and using it to challenge a lot of the conventional thinking that was going on internally," Bowen explains.

"And as a result of that, we were able to adopt much of the methodology and its values: iterative development, a keen focus on customer needs and rapid-fire releases, for example.

We managed to break through a lot of the internal bureaucracy that had previously made our solutions complex, or complete failures."

It became clear to us that at News Corp, the 3wks methodology wasn't simply being used to create and deploy products. In fact, that was its secondary function. Its primary objective was to ignite some sort of epiphany and cultural change within the company's tech and product teams. People and culture, Bowen believes, can make or break an organisation - especially an organisation going through a transformation.

"The 3wks methodology doesn't just work because it delivers great outcomes," she explains. "For us, the real value is the emphasis it puts on the pace and urgency of delivering value for customers."

"Most organisations going through a transformation struggle to translate their strategy into actions and outcomes. There's lots of deep, introspective discussions about how to respond to challenges, and those discussions turn into well-documented plans, PowerPoints, forums and all of those things. They never actually translate into actions and outcomes that a customer can meaningfully respond to.

So what we saw in the 3wks methodology was a sense of urgency that ensures what you're doing is deeply relevant to the customer. That was game changing."

Much like Woods, Bowen had used the 3wks methodology as a catalyst for accelerating News Corp's digital transformation. It was less about speeding up the delivery of products and more about effecting widespread cultural change. It became a tool for creating an environment in which developers felt empowered and productive, and a tool for instilling what Bowen saw as 'basic values' into the fabric of the organisation.

"The things that the 3wks methodology values, like direct connection to users, aren't particularly new," she claims.

"Many of the foundational practices that the 3wks methodology evangelises are pretty basic. Understanding (with clarity and purpose) what outcome you're trying to deliver is something all organisations should be doing. The other things - being unwavering in your persistence, not compromising your understanding of who the customer is, and being clear on who you're delivering an outcome to - are also not new.

In my opinion these are just basic principles should be fundamental to any organisation but unfortunately, many organisations have a habit of trying to squash them out. Introducing them into a place like News Corp is one challenge, but making them stick is another."

So Bowen and Drasutis had successfully exposed their teams to the less-than-revolutionary 3wks methodology, and had done so with the goal of changing the way they conceptualise and solve problems. But how were they making the change stick?

Like Woods, Bowen realised that the organisation needed to begin building its own internal capabilities. To keep the momentum going, she had to find a sustainable way of working that didn't rely on external providers, vendors or consultants. She had to make what was then an emerging culture survive in the long run.

Every organisation, Bowen says, can be Agile. But not every organisation can achieve the same standards of agility and individual empowerment as certain teams or businesses, and they shouldn't try to.

This is a striking opinion, and one that contrasts with the likes of Andrew Hunt who claims that Agile is dead precisely because organisations haven't stayed true to the creed set forth in the Agile Manifesto. Instead they have practised their own heretical versions of Agile, to the (perceived) destruction of Agile itself - something we fear could happen to the 3wks methodology.

Bowen isn't bothered by these sorts of statements and seems to dismiss the supposed schism between purists and pragmatists. She also ignores the suggestion that purism is the key to a methodology's survival:

"When we started our journey towards Agile somebody told me that the enemy of achieving an outcome was methodological purism," she says. "You can't be a perfectionist or a purist if you want to get something done."

"I think every organisation needs to find the right level or type of Agile that works for them. We all face constraints - functional constraints, market conditions, whatever else - and often those constraints are non-negotiable.

Some organisations, like 3wks, have the luxury of not being encumbered by too many constraints of that nature. But the rest of us aren't, and we just need to find a way to make it work. We need to adapt the methodology to our environment and go from there.

Doing that, I think, is better than doing nothing at all."

She was right. Rather than force-feed News Corp a methodology that it couldn't reasonably follow or sustain, Bowen had looked for something that could stick. Sure, the organisation wasn't practising Agile or 3wks proper, but it was still pushing the boundaries and changing how it worked. It was a pragmatic move.

"We invested in training, coaching, tools and collaboration platforms to make our version of the 3wks methodology as good as it can be," Bowen explains.

"After a few projects we understood how the 3wks methodology works in its purest form, and how we could make it our own."

At this point, she's clear in her assertion that 'going full 3wks' is not something News Corp - and organisations like it - should aspire towards.

"I think the 3wks methodology is impractical at scale for an organisation like News Corp that has certain accountabilities. And an army of 3wks companies would be chaos."

Large organisations, Bowen explains carefully, need a range of roles and personalities to be functional. The reality of working in complex organisations is that there isn't always space or opportunity for autonomy and boundary-pushing.

"But that doesn't mean that powerful new ideas, like the 3wks methodology, don't have a role to play," she adds.

"Any successful new way of thinking or doing things is further proof that we can deliver faster, better. And that's essential."

News Corp had proved to us that purism is indeed a fruitless pursuit, and that questions of methodological longevity are irrelevant. If the 3wks methodology has to adapt to fit an organisation, so be it. Getting things done is always the main goal. After all, digital innovation is for those who believe that doing is the best strategy.

Is fast the new future?

I t's been more than fifteen years since the Agile Manifesto was published, and five years since we started 3wks. Over this time, we've seen the software industry undergo a tremendous amount of change - and that change has well and truly infiltrated the broader business world.

"Software has eaten the world," writes Jeff Gothelf in the *Harvard Business Review*.

"And as it continues to consume new and diverse industries it's transforming the way business is done. We are all in the 'software business' now, regardless of the product or service we provide, forcing us to reexamine how we structure and manage our organisations."

Gothelf's assertions about the unstoppable influence of software are far from hyperbole. There are currently more than eighteen million software developers worldwide, and that number is expected to increase by forty-five per cent to twenty-six million in 2019. Parallel to that, organisations are increasingly focusing on delivering products, services and customer experiences through technology; and in doing so, they're transforming themselves into ersatz technology companies that worship at the altar of Agile.

We're seeing this happen even in the most slow-moving, heavily regulated corners of the business world, such as the banking and financial services industries. In early 2017, the Australian and New Zealand Banking Group (more commonly known as ANZ) announced its plans to 'blow up bureaucracy' and introduce Agile across its divisions in what is considered 'a huge culture change programme.' Huge doesn't begin to describe the scale of change that will have to happen at ANZ to transition it from a process-laden financial behemoth to a nimble, focussed organisation. But it's all the pursuit of 'getting things done,' says CEO Shayne Elliot.

General Electric is another mammoth organisation that has transformed

itself into a de facto tech company. In 2015, the multinational conglomerate effectively rebranded itself as a 'digital industrial company' (whatever that means) with a focus on creating digitally enabled products. As part of this transformation the company launched GE Digital, a twenty thousand-strong organisational unit that includes software developers and IT professionals. The unit, according to Brad Surak, GE Digital's Chief Operating Officer, has embraced Scrum and as a result been able to simplify administrative processes, solve pricing issues, improve communication across General Electric's businesses and more. Hallelujah!

The list of surprising and unlikely Agile devotees goes on. In the United States, National Public Radio (NPR) began using Agile methods in what it calls 'iterative programming.' Instead of investing millions in developing, launching and marketing big programmes, the network now creates cheap pilots of shows and effectively beta-tests them on groups of listeners. One study ranked NPR as the fifth most Agile company in the US, ahead of Google, Apple and Microsoft.

John Deere and Bank of America Merrill Lynch have also undergone sweeping digital transformations, injecting a hefty dose of Agile into their cultures and operations. Car manufacturers are getting on board too: General Motors has been on a transformation journey for years now, trying to introduce Agile in a bid to deliver innovations faster and shorten the time between vehicle design and manufacturing.

Everyone, it seems, doesn't just want to be better. They want to be *faster*. It's all about pace.

But is fast really the new future? Are we really moving on from our old ways?

Keep calm and fail fast

In 2011, the multi-hyphenate executive coach Ryan Babineaux joined Stanford Continuing Studies (Stanford University's programme for non-degree adult students) as an instructor. There he met Dr. John Krumboltz, the University's Professor of Education and Psychology, and together they created the highly popular course called 'Do It Anyway: Creating a Life of Passionate Action.'

The point of the six-week course, according to the official outline, was 'to provide an introduction to the Happenstance Approach, a way of living based on exploration, growth and embracing the unexpected.'

The Happenstance Approach is Babineaux's hallmark approach to career counselling, and it draws heavily on Krumboltz's work on happenstance learning theory (HLT). Writing in the *Journal of Career Assessment*, Krumboltz explains:

"In a nutshell, the HLT posits that human behaviour is the product of countless numbers of learning experiences made available by both planned and unplanned situations in which individuals find themselves. The learning outcomes include skills, interests, knowledge, beliefs, preferences, sensitives, emotions and future actions."

The HLT advances an approach to professional life that helps individuals benefit - not just cope with - unplanned events like failure. For Babineaux and Krumboltz, success isn't about whether you did something right or wrong. It's about what you learned in the process.

This concept eventually become known by the moniker 'fail fast, fail often' after Babineaux and Krumboltz's book, *Fail Fast, Fail Often: How Losing Can Help You Win*. In the book they describe the philosophy behind failing fast and failing often, arguing that the the most successful people tend to spend less time planning and more time 'doing' than others. Successful people, they say, get out into the world, try things, make mistakes and fail. They lay the foundation for future success by first finding out what works and what doesn't, benefiting from unexpected experiences and opportunities on the way. It's simple: if you're not experiencing failure, you're not trying hard enough.

The dictum 'fail fast, fail often' quickly gripped Silicon Valley and spread faster than an infection. Failure became a bizarre yardstick for success, and overnight everyone seemed to be eager to publicise all the times they'd failed.

Medium became awash with articles written by founders and entrepreneurs all too happy to tell the story of their most recent epic fail. A global conference called FailCon, now held in over a dozen cities spread across six continents, launched with the goal of giving startup founders a space 'to learn from and prepare for failure, so they can iterate and grow fast.' Meanwhile Fuckup Nights, an event series (or 'global movement') that provides a platform for professionals to tell their stories of failure, took off across the globe. From its website:

"Each month, in events across the globe, we get three to four people to get up in front of a room full of strangers to share their own professional fuckup. The stories of the business that crashes and burns, the partnership deal that goes sour, the product that has to be recalled, we tell them all."

We've now reached the point where even non-tech organisations outside of the Valley have gotten on the fast fail train. In Australia, Domino's Pizza has adopted lean and Agile methodologies as the norm and deliberately built a 'fast fail' culture into the organisation. Teams are encouraged to ditch business cases in favour of low-cost testing and experimentation.

"If you're spending time on building a business case before you have proved there is consumer interest in your idea via a small scale test, you're not failing fast," says Michael Gillespie, Group Chief Digital Officer at Domino's Pizza.

"Opinions need to be validated. You can test the concept of a large project for as little as $1,000."

Starbucks is another often-cited case study in fast failure outside of Silicon Valley. In 2010, the coffee chain added beer, wine and a selection of small plate items to its evening menu. The idea was to create a casual after-hours meeting environment where people could socialise, drink and be merry. The rationale? People who like coffee tend to also like beer and wine.

The problem, they realised, was that nobody who wants a beer thinks of Starbucks as a place to get it. Moreover, there was little demand for alcoholic beverages from Starbucks customers, many of whom use the chain as a virtual office, a study spot, or a place to get a quick caffeine hit.

Realising they'd failed, the global chain pulled the evening menu from most of its company-owned locations in the United States and decided to integrate beer and wine into its higher-end retail format, such as its Roastery stores. So far that idea hasn't proven to be a failure, but it's early days.

The idea of failing fast and failing often has become synonymous with the software industry and Silicon Valley, but also with 'innovative companies' and Agile. Of course, the Agile Manifesto makes no mention of failure. The closest it comes is in its commitment to 'responding to change over following a plan' and the underlying principle of continuous development. Linking the concept of 'fail fast, fail often' with Agile is a bit of a conceptual stretch.

But that doesn't stop anyone. Gov.uk, the website of the United

Kingdom's public sector (created by the Government Digital Service), lists the adage as one of the 'core principles of Agile' in its official Service Manual. The manual, designed to help government teams create and maintain digital services, says that services must be built using any Agile methods as long as they adhere to these core principles: focus on user needs, deliver iteratively, keep improving how your team works, keep planning, and fail fast and learn quickly.

"You should learn to fail and create a culture that learns from failure," the Service Manual proclaims, because "Agile techniques don't guarantee success."

The 'fail fast, fail often' mantra has come a long way from Stanford University, and it's probably safe to say that most organisations involved in software development or service delivery have jumped on its bandwagon. This self-professed propensity to quickly bounce back from failure is, one could argue, suggest that fast really is the new future. If organisations as varied as the UK public sector, Starbucks and Domino's Pizza are living life in the fast lane, then so is everyone else.

There's just one problem: there's no way to know whether these companies are actually experiencing productive failure and learning anything from it. When Rita Gunther McGrath, a professor at Columbia Business School, asks executives to rate how effective their organisations are at learning from failure on a scale from one to ten, she often gets a sheepish "two - or maybe three" as a response. Organisations and human beings in general are profoundly biased against failure, according to Gunther McGrath, and we typically make no systematic effort to study it and learn from it.

And there's another problem with the fast fail concept: everyone seems to have their own definition of 'fast.' It took seven years for Starbucks to take booze off its menu, but that's considered a fast fail in some circles. What's the benchmark for a truly fast fail? How fast is fast? And how quickly do you have to respond to a failure to make it 'a fast fail'?

The inherent problem with the 'fast fail' movement is that it doesn't provide an actual roadmap for learning from failure. In the glib pursuit of failure, organisations and entrepreneurs have opened themselves up to 'getting things wrong' and 'celebrating mistakes' with the naive assumption that the experience alone will, somehow, help them do better next time. But it doesn't.

In 2009 Paul A. Gompers, Professor of Business Administration at the Harvard Business School, posed the question: does failure really breed new knowledge or experience that can be leveraged into performance the second time around? In some cases, he says, it can. But over all, failure poses no significant benefit in terms of future performance.

This was the subject of a study Gompers conducted with a group of his peers at Harvard. The study looked at the behaviour and success of more than eight thousand entrepreneurs between the years 1975 and 2000, and it found that failure is not a particularly effective teacher.

"There are some talented entrepreneurs who fail on the first time, learn and then succeed," says Gompers, "but that is not the rule." The deep-rooted belief in the power and value of failure comes from what he calls 'attribution bias' - in other words, people generalising from (purely anecdotal) success-after-failure stories.

For fast to be the new future, we need more than a belief in our ability to move on from failure. Writing for Forbes, Daniel Newman, analyst and CEO of Broadsuite Media Group, says that the most innovative and fast-failing companies are those that practise Agile and its related techniques, like rapid prototyping. And herein lies the real message: a mantra alone is not enough. An organisation, project or world that works and fails fast needs to be supported by a set of working practices that make it possible to detect and remedy failures early, and quickly. Organisations looking to *be faster* first need to hone their practice of lean and Agile methodologies, like the 3wks methodology. And they're not quite there yet.

A long way off

The 'future of Agile in the enterprise' was a hot topic of discussion at Agile Australia 2015, a conference that drew a crowd of over one thousand attendees. There, some of Australia's top CIOs were asked about their organisation's Agile journeys and whether or not they'd succeeded in going full Agile. Alisa Bowen, in her trademark style, gave an incredibly honest answer:

"I think we are a long way off being great at it," she said, recounting News Corp's experience with Agile.

"This is a style of working and an approach that really started in our technology organisation, and frankly, it failed."

Bowen's candid response was echoed by her fellow panellist, Commonwealth Bank of Australia CIO (now Executive General Manager) Pete Steel. Agile had found success at the bank, he said, but getting there had been a bumpy ride. Cameron Gough, General Manager of Australia Post's Digital Delivery Centre, admitted that the postal services organisation had too suffered a number of setbacks on its ongoing Agile journey. Many mistakes were made and getting buy-in for Agile projects was difficult. There was still a long way to go, and more work to be done.

These experiences reflect something we already know and have addressed in this book. Yes, many organisations have become more lean and more nimble, but they've done so by embracing a grotesque version of Agile. Darrel K. Rigby, Jeff Sutherland and Hirotaka Tekuchi talked about this in the May 2016 issue of the *Harvard Business Review*.

"When we ask executives what they know about Agile, the response is usually an uneasy smile and a quip such as 'just enough to be dangerous.' They may throw around Agile-related terms ('sprints,' 'time boxes') and claim that their companies are becoming more and more nimble. But because they haven't gone through training, they don't really understand the approach. Consequently, they unwittingly continue to manage in ways that run counter to Agile principles and practices, undermining the effectiveness of Agile teams in units that report to them."

Even the organisations with the best intentions, the authors say, erode the benefits that Agile innovation can deliver. Fast is the new future - everyone is saying so - but few people have quite worked out how to make fast work.

Research published in the Dimension Data Global Customer Experience (CX) Benchmarking Report further proves this point. Digital innovation, the data shows, is happening at a snail's pace. According to Dimension Data:

- Eighty-seven per cent of organisations rate their customer experience delivery as 'poor';
- Only fifty-one per cent of organisations have a digital strategy' and
- Of those that do have a digital strategy, ten per cent believe the strategy is optimised.

If the numbers are anything to go by, we're a long way off from a fast future. Many organisations are still grappling with Agile, and they're struggling with large-scale cultural shifts and making Agile 'stick.' This is why people like Alisa Bowen and Cameron Gough are focusing so much on *people and change*. If they want to be fast, resilient and productive, they need to get the culture right first.

Talking about how Australia Post used an Agile methodology to develop its post office locator application, Gough recounts his difficulty in getting Agile off the ground:

"It was a nice and neat, simple architecture and we nailed it," he said. "But once the celebration died down, we took a look at it and said 'actually we really didn't get anything out of this, and...We didn't see any uplift in our Agile capability.

It was an 'aha moment' about how we create the environment and culture in which Agile can grow and prosper. That was a big shift for us, and from that movement we moved away from focusing on doing Agile and how to create an environment in which Agile can survive."

Gough's experience cuts to the essence of what it takes to become 'fast.' Recruiting and developing talent, investing in coaching and facilitating training is essential for getting teams adjusted to change and comfortable with a new methodology, whether that's Agile or something else. It's also important for putting a stop to the self-sabotaging behaviours of executives who know 'just enough' Agile buzzwords 'to be dangerous.'

Organisations can fundamentally make a difference in how they doing things if they have lieutenants around them who are able - and willing - to execute ideas quickly, bounce back from failure and iterate. The importance of ability and willingness here can't be overstated. At Monash University, Trevor Woods has a team of people who get to work every day and just do. They don't spend endless amounts of time talking about what they're going to do, how they're going to do it or when they're going to do it. They just crack on with the task and go from there. And that attitude is what makes them successful.

Being fast and resilient is, at the end of the day, a cultural thing. Organisations can wax lyrical about how Agile they are or how often they 'fail fast', but without the right attitudes - at both management and team level - the future won't be fast. For the future to be fast, organisations need to work on things like:

- Accepting responsibility for outcomes

- Valuing delivery over perfection

- Creating an environment in which fast is possible

But how can they do that? The 3wks methodology is one way. Using it forces organisations to commit to outcomes and organise themselves in a way that breaks down information silos and enables a continuous feedback loop. At a fundamental level, the 3wks methodology makes organisations control the innate human need to control and plan, and instead become more resilient and adaptable. The question, however, is if that's *really* doable.

Another paradigm

On the 29th May 1953, Sir Edmund Hillary and Tenzing Norgay became the first people to reach the summit of Mount Everest, Earth's highest mountain.

It was an incredible achievement, especially given that a number of previous expeditions - many of them British - had tried and failed to ascend the infamous mountain before. When news of Hillary and Norgay's success broke around the world (on the day of Queen Elizabeth II's coronation, no less), the pair were hailed as as an inspiration for all Britons. Hillary, a humble beekeeper from New Zealand, and Norgay, a Nepali Sherpa, had captured the imaginations of people worldwide with their daring and conquest.

What imagination and popular history failed to realise, however, was that the heroic two were part of an expedition organised under the command of Colonel John Hunt. Their party included some of Britain's best climbers and a score of highly experienced Sherpas - including Norgay, who had been participating in British attempts to climb Everest since the 1930s. The entire expedition was carefully planned, and its members were armed with state of the art equipment including portable radios, insulated boots and closed-circuit oxygen systems. Imagined in the context of this well-managed project, Hillary and Norgay's historic achievement still seems incredible, but it loses some of its mystique.

Patrick Hollingworth recalls the famed 1953 expedition in his book, *The Light and Fast Organisation*:

"The British Mount Everest Expedition in 1953 was conducted very much like a military campaign; it was led by the British Army's Colonel John Hunt, and took five months to complete. The total expedition party comprised 400 people, with seven camps placed on the mountain, and it was only at the end of the fourth month that they were ready to make their summit push."

Hollingworth, a mountaineer himself, cites the 1953 expedition as a classic example of the 'traditional approach' to mountaineering. This approach, which he calls the 'expedition style', is to mountaineering what waterfall is to software development: old school, time consuming and resource-intensive.

"It's a style," Hollingworth writes "that involves lots of people, lots of equipment, lots of energy and lots of time to overpower the challenges of the mountain."

According to Hollingworth, expedition-style climbing remains the most dominant style of mountaineering today. It's the foundation for a multimillion-dollar commercial climbing industry, and its the style used in ninety per cent of climbs undertaken in Nepal.

Yet despite his criticism of the style, Hollingworth maintains that there are times where it does work. If the weather is cooperating and things go to plan, the expedition style delivers. Moreover, it "enables climbers deep in the pocket but light on skills a reasonable shot at summitting."

But when it doesn't work, it *really* doesn't work. If the stars don't align, the expedition style is a recipe for death on a large scale. Countless lives have been lost because mountaineers have overestimated their skills or the predictability of Everest itself. And therein lies the problem.

"At its core," Hollingworth explains "expedition style is all about people attempting to control and simplify an environment that is naturally volatile, uncertain and complex.

When things go to plan and the weather cooperates, it's a style that works. But when things go pear-shaped…they go pear-shaped in a pretty major way."

His description of traditional mountaineering bears an uncanny resemblance to 'traditional' software development and the business environment at large (which, incidentally, is the actual focus of his book). Waterfall, software's proverbial expedition style, has too seen its fair share of failure and carnage. Unbearably long projects, catastrophically blown budgets, bad products and failed launches; these are the hallmarks of a traditional software development methodology that is largely dysfunctional, but still widely practised.

Fortunately, software development has experienced a bout of methodological diversity and organisations are now practising Agile, or variants of it at least. Mountaineering, it seems, has developed a new style of climbing too. It's called the alpine style.

This style of mountaineering received one of its first written descriptions by Yvon Chouinard, the founder of the clothing company Patagonia, in his book *Climbing Ice*. Twenty years later it was given a more formal treatment in *Extreme Alpinism*, a book written by leading alpinist, Mark Twight, and James Martin. Writing on his blog, Hollingworth describes the alpine style as the antithesis of the expedition style:

"It involves fewer people, takes much less time, uses less energy and resources, and is generally structurally flat.

At its core, Alpine Style is all about people letting go of their innate need to control an environment…and instead responding according to the natural ebb and flow of changing conditions."

In his book, Hollingworth goes on to explain his model for helping organisations transition to the alpine style in a bid to get them responding better in situations of complexity and uncertainty. It's a difficult task: getting organisations to buy-in to the idea of the alpine style is one thing, but getting them to do it is another.

"Man of our expedition-style organisations are starting to recognise the benefits of the alpine-style approach - and they want in," he writes.

"But they are not really prepared to do the hard work. You'll be able to recognise them from their sudden adoption of corporate spin such as 'Agile' and 'innovative' into their organisational vocabulary."

The picture Hollingworth paints here - of buzzword-wielding corporate executives in open-plan offices bedecked with brightly coloured furniture - is one we see all the time in software. As it turns out, working in a way that challenges our innate need to control, plan and prepare is difficult. Whether it be in the mountains or in the office, human beings struggle to work light and fast. And while many people are eager to say they're 'failing fast!' and 'iterating rapidly!' or 'doing Agile', they're often not willing or able to actually *do* it. We must beware the expedition-style organisation in alpinists's clothing.

Hollingworth's Alpine Style Model helps transition organisations from the expedition to the alpine style, and it does so with a focus on key skills, insights and traits. If you want to move light and fast, looking like an alpinist, Hollingworth says, is not enough. You need to actually *be* one.

We won't describe Hollingworth's model in full. You can read about it in his own book, *The Light and Fast Organisation*. But here's the key takeaway: to really be light and fast, an organisation must have a specific set of skills, a specific set of traits or attitudes, a good understanding of its strengths, and consciously-designed teams. Being intentional in the way you structure teams, engage in dialogue and develop a growth-driven culture is essential if you ever want to get to the top of the mountain without needing a team of four hundred and a truckload of gear. And while it's a difficult process of introspection and cultural change, making the transition from expedition-style to alpine-style is entirely doable.

Fast, it seems *can* be the new future. But we have to be willing to work on ourselves first.

Fast forward

Paul Shetler, former head of the Australian Government's Digital Transformation Office, talks eloquently about the need for people's skills, mindsets and attitudes to change. The human factor, he says, plays an important part in practising Agile and delivering outcomes.

The problem, as we've seen, is that changing behaviours and countering internal biases is hard. It's easier to retreat into strategising and planning than it is to really go 'full alpine' or 'full 3wks.' Repeating a mantra like 'fail fast, fail often' is easier than actually building a framework for resilience, or an organisation that actually knows how to learn from a mistake. Organisations are, at the end of the day, just groups of people. And people are hard to change.

Donald H. McGannon, an American broadcasting executive who played a crucial role in the television industry's formative years, once said that leadership is action, not position. If we want fast to be the new future, then we simply have to be fast. Forget the slogans, the buzzwords and the mantras we use to position ourselves as fast. It's time to get back to the roots of Agile, change our behaviours and start working in a way that actually makes us fast.

The future, if we want it, is now.

Beyond Agile

Mark Twain (apparently) once said that the secret to getting ahead is getting started.

In the last chapter we asked ourselves if fast really is the future of software. The answer, we found, is yes - but only if organisations are willing and able to change.

Unfortunately, change is not something that comes naturally to human beings. We resist it on a fundamental level because many of us have a low tolerance for ambiguity and uncertainty. Often, we default to heuristics to make the task of coping with change a little bit easier. Other times we default to the status quo (some call this 'status quo bias') because comprehending change is just a bit too much.

Some of us also eschew change because we adhere to a common fallacy known as 'appeal to tradition' (or appeal to common practice). This appeal takes the all-too familiar form of 'this is the right thing to do because we've always done it this way.'

Research has shown that this is a rather commonly held fallacy. In fact, the results of a 2010 study published in the *Journal of Experimental Social Psychology* found that people, on the whole, have a tangible preference for things that simply appear older. In the study participants were presented with two university courses: an old existing course and a new, alternative one. Participants wholeheartedly preferred the former, and expressed even more enthusiasm for it when they were told it had been in existence for one hundred years, rather than only ten years.

They said the same thing when asked to rate acupuncture as a function of how old the practice was. They also preferred paintings that were older when compared with more modern works, and they liked a four thousand year old tree more than a five hundred year old tree - even though the trees were in fact the same.

For some people, age or 'time in existence' operates as a heuristic. The longer something has been around, the better it must be. *We've always done it this way.* This kind of longevity bias perhaps explains why some people are persistent in their belief that waterfall-style projects work or that Agile is still the future, despite its many well-documented instances of failure.

But how do we explain the existence and behaviours of allegedly cutting-edge CIOs and IT professionals who have jumped on the Agile bandwagon and ridden it to hashtag-digital transformation? Time in existence is a heuristic works both ways; for some, it means that older is better. For others, it's the opposite.

In 2015 Paul Cairns, a professor of human-computer interaction at the University of York, asked a group of people to play two rounds of *Don't Starve*, an adventure game in which players must collect objects using a map. In the first round, Cairns and his researchers told the group that the map would be randomly generated. In the second round, they said it would be determined and controlled by an 'adaptive' artificial intelligence (AI) that would change the map based on an individual player's skill level.

In reality, neither game used AI. But a survey conducted after both rounds showed that the players believed the supposed AI version of the game was more immersive, and more entertaining.

"The adaptive AI put me in a safer environment and seemed to present me with resources as needed," one player said. Another said it reduced the time required to explore the map, which made the game more fun.

Cairns repeated the experiment with a group of forty new subjects and experienced the same results. It turns out that people have higher opinions of things they think are 'new' or things that have been updated with new features. Speaking to *New Scientist*, Florida State University psychologist Water Boot says that the experiment proves that expectations influence people's experiences.

"The expectation is that something new must be better than the thing before," he says. "Maybe that's why people go with a new iPhone every few years."

It's maybe also why people were so quick to embrace Agile without fully understanding it first, and why people remain so dedicated to its variants (like Scrum).

Making ideas stick in today's fast-paced world is difficult business. In the face of new ideas, people either default to what they know (the 'older is better' camp) or quickly get on board with whatever is new and exciting. And while we've seen the number of software development methodologies proliferate over the past fifty years, we haven't really seen a proportionate rise in innovation or even uptake of methodologies that truly break with the waterfall paradigm. We've had some brilliant ideas and explored new ways of working, but most organisations (even those practising Agile) are operating in the same old ways. The Agile Manifesto is only a few years shy of being twenty years old, and yet few organisations have truly understood and adopted its principles. Why? And will the 3wks methodology suffer the same fate?

In this last chapter, we'll explore what drives change in software development methodology, and what it will take for us to really change. In doing so, we hope to synthesise the contents of this book and give you - our reader - the tools you need to really go beyond Agile.

A community in crisis

Robert Shiller, renowned economist and Nobel Laureate, explores the pace of innovation vis-à-vis the pace of research and ideas in his 2005 working paper, *Behavioral Economics and Institutional Innovation.*Unpacking the role behavioural economics has historically played in innovation at the firm level, Shiller notes that while theorising is a steady business, innovation is not.

"Those who would like to see their economic theories embodied in new institutions may have to wait many years to see that happen," he writes.

"One reason that innovation seems so episodic is that it tends to be spurred by major economic crises, and can take place only in the rare times when the public perceives an urgent need for change."

Here, Shiller presents crises - not ideas, methodologies or manifestos - as the chief catalysts for innovation. This isn't a new concept by any means; for decades, economists and social scientists have talked about 'creative destruction,' 'shock adjustment,' 'paradigm shifts' and 'punctuated equilibrium' to explain the disruptive and transformative impact of things like war and technological advancement. Stephen Krasner, Professor of International Studies at Stanford University, argues that new structures and institutions - both social and political - emerge in times of crisis, assuming a life of their own and "altering the basic nature of civil society itself."

What has this got to do with software? Everything. If we look at the evolution of software development methodology since the mid-twentieth century, it is possible to identify crisis points that correlate with methodological and ideological turning points.

Let's take the early days of software, for example. In the 1950s and 1960s (the era of Winston Royce and his contemporaries) software development was often compared to bridge building. Software, many argued, was predictable and inflexible in its design - just like a bridge. And that's why it was important to gather requirements and documentation up front; you can't change a bridge's design halfway through its construction.

This perceived affinity between software development and civil engineering somewhat made sense at the time. In those days, software was designed and built for the analog world. Developers were constrained by the limitations of the hardware they were working with, and many early software projects were geared towards exploiting that hardware to the fullest extent, often to automate existing paper-based processes within organisations. Albert Endres explored this in his presentation *A Synopsis of Software Engineering History: The Industrial Perspective*, delivered at the Dagstuhl-Seminar 9635 in 1996. Referring to the period between 1956 and 1967, Endres explained:

"It is the era where the term 'software engineering' had not been coined yet…and the first computers that achieved significant use in the industry, be it for commercial or scientific applications were batch-oriented systems. This mode of operation resulted from the two typical I/O and storage media, namely punched cards and magnetic tape.

The main goal of software development was to exploit the limited hardware resources (storage and processing power) in an optimal way. Any less than optimal use could double or triple the processing times, measured in hours, or make the total job infeasible."

By the time the 1970s arrived, things had changed. New technologies and capabilities - like incremental compilation, source-level editing and debugging - had emerged and the industry found itself in the midst of a 'software crisis.' William Aspray, professor of information technologies at the University of Texas in Austin, highlights two possible causes of this particular crisis:

1. **Technology imbalance**. During the 1960s, memory and processor speed increased markedly, but software development techniques didn't. The resulting imbalance between possibility and capability lead to a crisis in confidence.

2. **Expectations**. With the advancement in technology came heightened expectations. More was expected of operating systems and software programmes in the late 1960s and 1970s than ever before, and developers had difficulty meeting these expectations.

Other possible causes of the software crisis include simple economics (more and more people were commissioning development projects and wanting to control them rigidly) and plain old rhetoric; a few large-scale, dramatic failures (such as the IBM OS/360 and the Mariner I spacecraft failure of 1962) might have led to the belief that there was a software crisis unfolding.

Whatever its cause, the crisis marked a turning point in the industry's methodological history. Suddenly, the industry was consumed with the need to reduce development risks, raise productivity and improve the quality of software. By 1968 attendees of the NATO Software Engineering Conference in Germany had announced that the software crisis was well and truly underway, and two years later Royce's seminal paper *Managing the Development of Large Software Systems* was published. A new era in software development had begun, and it was characterised by SDLC methodologies and wasteful, requirements-driven processes. You can refer back to chapters three and four to see how that all worked out.

In the aftermath of that first major crisis point, the software industry seemed to find its footing. The 1980s saw computers continue to advance in processing power and capability, and (as Endres argues) this was the era in which the traditional dominance of hardware over software ended. The change in the hardware environment, namely the spread of CRT displays and graphical user interface (GUI) tools, gave programmers more power and capability. The constraints had been lifted and it seemed like anything was possible.

Except it wasn't. In 1987 the California Department of Motor Vehicles (DMV) in the United States embarked upon a major application redevelopment project to 'revitalise' its drivers license and registration application processes. The primary reason behind the project, according to the DMV, was to embrace new technologies:

> *"The specific objective of the 1987 project was to use modern technology to support the DMV mission and sustain its growth by strategically positioning the DMV data processing environment to rapidly respond to change."*

By 1993, the projected had been cancelled and there was no new drivers license and registration application programme to show for it. A total of $45 million dollars (around $76 million in today's money) had been spent.

The California DMV's story was just one of many surfacing around that time. It seemed that by the 1990s, the software industry was in the midst of yet another crisis. The 1994 edition of the Chaos Report published by The Standish Group revealed some disturbing facts:

- The average cost of a development project at a large company was $2,322,000 (about $3, 760, 000 in today's money);

- More than thirty per cent of projects were canceled before they were completed;

- Nearly sixty per cent of projects were expected to cost one 189 per cent above original estimates - and that doesn't include lost opportunity costs; and

- On average, just sixteen per cent of software projects were completed on time and on budget. That number was small as nine per cent for large companies.

Based on these findings The Standish Group estimated that in 1995, American companies and government bodies would spend $81 billion on cancelled software projects, plus an additional $59 million on projects that would be completed over time and/or budget.

Though they painted a disturbing picture, the figures reported in the now-infamous Chaos report were mirrors that the software industry could not avoid. Discussions about why projects fail or succeed began to dominate public discourse. Off the back of its original research, The Standish Group surveyed IT executive managers for their view on what made a project successful. Project success, it seemed, came down to three critical factors:

user involvement, support from executive management, and clearly stated requirements. Interestingly, further research by The Standish Group found that "smaller time frames, with delivery of software components early and often" increased the success of projects.

It was around the time of this 'project failure' crisis that new software development methodologies, like extreme programming, began to emerge. Once again, programmers were forced to innovate in response to a crisis and challenged by the need to deliver better software on budget and on time, they experimented with new ways of working and managing projects. This gave rise to methodologies like XP, FDD, Crystal Clear and eventually Agile. The rest, as they say, is history.

So here we are. Software development methodology has undoubtedly been shaped by crises, as Shiller and others would expect, and as a result we've progressed from wasteful SDLC methodologies like waterfall to practising the comparatively lean Agile methodologies. But, as we've discussed in this book, those methodologies are failing us too.

We're in the middle of another crisis, but this time it's an institutional one that isn't isolated to the software industry alone. According to Lucy Loh and Patrick Hoverstadt (authors of *The Fractal Organization and Patterns of Strategy*) we're in the midst of a wider business failure epidemic:

"Of the five hundred companies that started the Standard & Poor's index, eighty-five per cent failed to survive forty years - less than the working life of the people in them - and these figures pre-date the 2007/08 crisis," they write.

"Only one of the original five hundred remain."

Company mortality rates are at an all-time high. In 2015, researchers at the Santa Fe Institute in New Mexico found the average life expectancy of publicly-traded firms in the United States to be just ten years, taking into account acquisitions, mergers and bankruptcy. In that same year, the Boston Consulting Group (BCG) conducted a study of more than thirty thousand listed companies in the US and found that the lifespan of companies has decreased significantly since 1950, and businesses now move through their lifecycles twice as quickly as they did thirty years ago. Moreover, companies aren't just dying younger; they're also more likely to perish at any time. Nearly one-tenth of all public companies fail each year, a fourfold increase since 1965. Today, there's just a *one-in-three chance* that your business will survive the next five years.

What's to blame for this mortality crisis? Sample size could be one factor. There are more businesses now than there have been in the past and statistically, this could push mortality rates up. Another popular theory is that certain types of companies and industries, such as the technology industry, account for most of the shift in company life expectancy. The Boston Consulting Group calls nonsense on this, though. According to their research, mortality risk has grown uniformly across all sectors of the economy, and across companies of different sizes and ages. Industry has little to do with it.

In reality, corporate longevity is determined by a myriad of factors and the roots of the mortality crisis, therefore, are varied. Writing in the *McKinsey Quarterly*, former McKinsey managing director Ian Davis says that the cause of business demise includes failure to effectively address changes in market demand or competition; human failings such as hubris, exhaustion or loss of ambition; and, above all, an inability to deal with new, disruptive technological innovations. But these aren't the leading cause of business failure.

"Perhaps less commented upon," Davis writes "is the challenge presented by legacy assets and legacy mind-sets."

"A failure to adapt to seismic change (whether customer or technology driven) is, I have found, rarely caused by intellectual oversights or an inability to grasp what is happening.

More often, the culprit is an inability to escape from a successful past and to accept the huge financial and human costs of responding effectively."

Davis's insight gets to the heart of why Agile has failed and why, in an era characterised by unprecedented business failure, the software industry isn't adapting or changing. Organisations are trying to cope with disruption by a thousand startups (or what Paul Shetler calls hypercompetition) and using Agile to do it, but they've been unable to overcome the tremendous power of legacy thinking and practise Agile the way its founders intended. Instead of actually adopting Agile practices, managers have largely relied on what Patrick Hoverstadt calls 'tacit' organisational models - models that they themselves have built up over a lifetime - to run development projects and solve problems. They've waved the Agile flag but largely stuck to what they know because, as Davis points out, changing your ways can be costly and emotionally demanding. It's all just a bit too hard.

We realised things were bad in the 1990s, and that something had to change if we hoped to deliver projects on time and on budget. However, the results of the The Standish Group Chaos report since 1994 show marginal change over the past twenty years. On average:

- Just twenty-nine per cent of projects tend to succeed in delivering functionality on time and on budget;

- Nearly fifty per cent of projects do not meet scope, time or budget expectations; and

- More than twenty per cent of projects fail entirely and are canceled.

If we were to chart The Standish Group's findings over a twenty-year period, we'd have ourselves a flat trend line. To quote Alan Zucker of Fannie Mae, "we are no better at delivering a project today than we were twenty years ago."

What it will take to change

The software development community (and human beings more broadly) are, evidently, not very good at changing or evolving. We've made very little progress in the last twenty years and software projects are still cumbersome, wasteful and expensive.

So what must organisations do to truly move beyond Agile?

1. Culture

As the speed of business cycles continues to increase - and the average lifespan of a business declines - innovation is becoming even more critical to growth.

But while eighty-four per cent of global executives (canvassed as part of McKinsey's Global Innovation Survey) agree that innovation is important to their company's growth strategy, only six per cent of them are satisfied with their company's innovation performance.

What's more, most executives don't know why their organisations aren't innovative. They also don't know how to go about fixing that or encouraging innovative ideas. Incubators, hackathons and rewards programmes just aren't cutting it.

But here's the thing: being innovative has almost nothing to do with having innovative ideas. Being innovative is about being open to innovation, and creating a culture in which innovation and creativity can thrive.

The link between organisational culture and innovation has been studied extensively in academic circles. Writing in the *Journal of Product Innovation Management*, researchers from Justus Liebig University Giessen reviewed some forty-three individual studies on the subject matter alone. According to their meta-review, there is indeed a causal relationship between culture and innovation in organisations. They found that the relationship between organisational culture and innovation *generation* is stronger than the relationship between organisational culture and innovation *adoption*. That is, your company's culture has more of an impact on your ability to generate innovative ideas than your ability to adopt them.

So the first thing you need to do to move beyond Agile and embrace the 3wks methodology is work on your company's culture. The importance of company culture on performance is often overstated in literature, but here we can't stress it enough. You cannot move fast and innovate if innovation is not built-in as part of your culture.

But how can you meaningfully make innovation a part of your culture? David Kester, former chief executive of the Design Council, has a few tips. The first is to look outside.

"Those businesses that are going to be the most successful," Kester says "are going to be drawing (new) ideas from the market."

"They're not going to be looking inwards and thinking that they've got it."

In their quest to become innovative, many companies inadvertently become introspective. They host internal innovation workshops, put up 'ideas wikis' and encourage employees to share their ideas. This is fine, but it doesn't achieve much in the way of actually creating a culture that is amenable to innovation. Instead, companies should be looking outwards and drawing their ideas directly from customers and stakeholders, working collaboratively with them in the process.

A great example of this was Trevor Woods's 'pop-up' innovation project (refer back to Chapter Six for a refresher) in which he gave the 3wks team a week to find and solve a problem for Monash University students. Instead of looking inward for a problem to solve and a product to build, he put us out on campus and had us talking directly with students to discover what they were feeling, doing and experiencing. We had a product built within days.

This, according to Ian Davis, is one of the hallmarks of adaptive and resilient companies. "These companies," Davis explains "avoid introversion and actively seek to understand broader trends outside their own organisations and industries."

But here's where Kester's second piece of advice comes in. You can't just spend all your time in the field, taking on each idea and problem you come across. It would spell financial ruin for your company, and probably damage your reputation in the process. To create a culture of innovation, you need *discipline*.

"You've got to do it in a disciplined way," says Kester. You need a rigorous process for conceptualising and understanding problems, and you need to be prototyping and testing solutions in controlled environments. Innovation is not a free-fall; it requires control, within reason. Having a process (or a methodology like ours) is the difference between simply responding to a problem and innovating.

The third way to embed innovation in your company culture, Kester says, is to bring in the outsiders.

"You can actually introduce some animators into the business," he explains.

"Outside individuals often have a perspective and they're connectors across different worlds. They can be very, very helpful, particularly when you're trying to move an innovation piece forward."

This tactic is straight out of the pages of Alisa Bowen's book. In Chapter Seven we recounted our experience with News Corp, where Bowen had us performing the role of the cat among the pigeons. She had used 3wks as a catalyst for accelerating her company's transformation from siloed stalwart to innovation machine; it was less about speeding up the delivery of products and more about effecting widespread cultural change. Our role as outsiders wasn't to provide an extra pair of hands here or there. Our job was to provide a different perspective and move innovation forward.

There's more to innovation than just having new ideas. Being innovative is about discipline, perspective and encouraging variety in ideas. Brian Leavy, AIB Professor of Strategic Management at Dublin City University Business School, puts it eloquently:

"Turning ideas into commercial reality requires persistence and discipline, and overall effectiveness ultimately depends on management being able to find the right balance between corporate creativity and efficiency."

So as you embark upon your digital transformation journey and work towards a future beyond Agile, remember this: your culture matters. You will not be able to move fast and survive the next five years without making innovation a part of who you are on a cultural level. And to do that, you need to be customer-centric, disciplined and willing to work with outsiders.

2. People and skills

People are the second thing you need to move beyond Agile. But not just any people; you need people with the right skills, values and attitudes.

Writing in *The Mythical Man-Month: Essays on Software Engineering*, Fred Brooks said that people are everything. "The quality of the people on a project and their organisation and management," he explained "are much more important factors in success than the tools they use or the technical approaches they take."

In the days of yore, people working on software development projects were specialists tasked with executing discrete tasks. Business analysts created requirements documents, systems analysts translated those requirements into specifications, programmers wrote code according to those specifications, and testers evaluated that code. Each person had an individual role to play along the software assembly line.

Things have changed considerably since then. And while it's important to still have specialists among your ranks, you need to shift your focus to viewing people as resources (not cogs in a machine) with wide potential. This means you need people who are generalists as well as specialists, and people who are dedicated to continuous learning. Moreover, you need organisational policies that enable Agile-esque practices.

Inevitably, people and processes vary considerably between different organisations; what's right for your company might not be right for another. That said, here are some guidelines to follow:

- Create small, high-performance teams and let them set their own objectives from the get-go;

- Resist the temptation to add people to those small teams, even in large-scale projects. As Fred Brooks said, adding manpower to a late software project just makes it later;

- Use a fractal organisational model to scale teams and projects, and to allow all groups and functions within your company to interact directly with customers;

- Hire experts and generalists, not managers and worker bees;

- Encourage and train people of all skill levels to engage with customers. Don't hide developers behind project managers;

- Establish role clarity. Don't isolate and segment people based purely on function and skill, but make sure they understand what outcomes they're responsible for; and

- Set time-boxed expectations and aim for an eighty per cent success rate. This sets clear, achievable goals for project teams.

This sounds like a lot of HR hokum, but it's important. Just as it is in a professional kitchen, *mise en place* is critical for creating a resilient software development operation that is capable of moving beyond Agile.

3. Strategy

Strategy is an oft-abused term in the literature on digital transformation and Agile. LinkedIn, Medium and other publishing platforms are awash with articles on 'how to develop your digital transformation strategy' and 'why strategy is important.' Much of it is nauseating.

But though it is an exhausted concept, strategy is important. If you're going to make the move beyond Agile, you need a strategy to pull it off.

We can turn to Michael Porter's seminal 1996 Harvard Business Review article What is Strategy? for a refresher on what a 'strategy' actually is. According to Porter, 'strategising' is the creation of a unique and viable business position involving:

- **Few** needs of **many** customers

- **Broad** needs of **few** customers

- **Broad** need of **many** customers in a **narrow** market

This approach forces us to make decisions and critically evaluate trade-offs. These trade-offs help us to identify 'fit,' which Porter argues is a source of competitive advantage. Long story short, organisations can't rely on operational efficiency or 'best practices' to get something - like a project or digital transformation - done. They need to be deliberate about choosing which activities and priorities to focus on, and combining those activities into a system.

So to move beyond Agile, you need a strategy. And that strategy can't just be 'embrace Agile values' or 'introduce daily stand-up meetings and an open office plan.' It's not enough to benchmark your own performance against your competitors and focus on 'building efficiency' or 'improving productivity.' That's not a strategy for anything, let alone one for going beyond Agile.

What you need a competitive strategy that actually gets you from Point A(gile) to Point B(eyond Agile). Ask yourself:

- What are our competitors doing? How can we do this *differently*?

- What *activities* do we need to do to meet some of the needs of a small subset of our user group?

- What do we need to do to meet *many* of the needs a small subset of our user group?

- How do we combine these activities? What are we willing to give up in pursuit of our goal?

- What are we *not* going to do?

These questions will help you get to the essence of your strategy, which is choosing what not to do. You may, for example, discover that your competitors are using Agile processes to deliver products to customers. Off the back of that, you decide that you will invest energy in prototyping and releasing products to small user groups, but you won't do it for every project.

All of this sounds a bit complicated, but it's not. The simple point behind Porter's approach to strategy is this: strategy is a tool for maintaining focus on objectives. Nothing more, nothing less. Having a clear picture of what you want and what you're prepared to do (and not do) to get it is essential for achieving any sort of goal, and for getting over internal barriers to change such as:

- Competing priorities

- Functional boundaries

- Poor vision or insufficient communication

- Change fatigue

If you're serious about going beyond Agile, you can't do it without a solid idea of why and how you're going to do it.

4. Infrastructure

The last thing you need to move beyond Agile is infrastructure. The premise is simple: you can't build, deploy and test quickly and iteratively without the right infrastructure.

That infrastructure, in our opinion, is the serverless cloud. Why? Because using a serverless cloud enables you to automate the provisioning and operation of your infrastructure; there are still servers, but you don't have to babysit them anymore.

This means you don't need a huge infrastructure team to support projects, and you don't need to operate a data centre. The result is some serious savings (and a shift from capital expenditure to operational expenditure) which can be better spent on value-creating projects, or rewarding your hardworking employees.

We won't labour this point, as we've explored it thoroughly in Chapter Five. But here's the bottom line: you can't expect your old infrastructure to support your new way of working. It won't. And in the off chance it does, it will cost you.

There's no time like the present

There's a lot of research and anecdotal evidence that proves that Agile methodologies and iterative software development processes are vastly superior to 'traditional' methodologies like waterfall. That goes without saying.

But if you learn only one thing from this book, let it be this: Agile is dead. Why? Because even though it's caught on like a California wildfire, Agile has become less of a framework and more of a Frankenstein's monster of practices and values that merely pay lip service to the original Agile Manifesto. Companies of all shapes and sizes have latched onto Agile and focused heavily on its ancillary characteristics, without ever bothering to understand and embrace its core message:

We are uncovering better ways of developing software by doing it and helping others do it. Through this work we have come to value:

- *Individuals and interactions* over processes and tools

- *Working software* over comprehensive documentation

- *Customer collaboration* over contract negotiation

- *Responding to change* over following a plan

We believe that these values, captured in the Agile Manifesto back in the early 2000s, are still important today. But Agile alone is not enough anymore. In the face of rapid change, technological advancement and ever-shortening business lifecycles, we need more. In the midst of a business failure crisis we can't afford to be tidsoptimists anymore; the world will leave us behind if we're not ready to make a change now. We need way to work that is rapid, productive and sustainable - and we needed it yesterday. We need to go beyond Agile.

Acknowledgements

A ndrew and Paul would like to thank the following for making this book a reality:

The 3wks team: Shane, Karin, Dave, Adrian M, Sean, Glenn, Martin, Marc, Kim, Sophia, Pete, Willis, Adrian F, Justin, Adam, Steve, Boony, Kosta, Nick, Matt, Rob, Ryan, Erika, Zane and Ingrid.

We'd also like to thank our amazing clients and the people who contributed so much to the creation of this book, particularly Grace and Nikola.

And last but not least our extraordinarily patient and loving families: Paul's - Dymphna, Becky and James. Andrew's - Alison, Amanda and Alex.

CPSIA information can be obtained
at www.ICGtesting.com
Printed in the USA
LVOW10*0000260917

550042LV00006B/86/P